RETIRE N.O.W.

(Not when **O**thers **W**ould)

A Comprehensive Guide to Retiring on **Your** Schedule

CHAD ENSIGN

Chad Ensign/Ensign Wealth Management
4447 E. Broadway
#101
Mesa, AZ 85206
https://ensignwm.com/

Book layout ©2020 Advisors Excel, LLC

The Complete Guide to Retirement/Chad Ensign. — 1st edition

ISBN 9798551114901

Chad Ensign is registered as an Investment Advisor Representative and is a licensed insurance agent in several states, including Utah, Arizona, and California (operating with California Insurance Licence No. 0K68065). Ensign Wealth Management is an independent financial services firm that helps individuals create retirement strategies using a variety of investment and insurance products to custom suit their needs and objectives.

Investment advisory services offered only by duly registered individuals through AE Wealth Management, LLC (AEWM). AEWM and Ensign Wealth Management are not affiliated companies. The appearances in Kiplinger were obtained through a PR program. 629871

The contents of this book are provided for informational purposes only and are not intended to serve as the basis for any financial decisions. Any tax, legal, or estate planning information is general in nature. It should not be construed as legal or tax advice. Always consult an attorney or tax professional regarding the applicability of this information to your unique situation.

Information presented is believed to be factual and up-to-date, but we do not guarantee its accuracy, and it should not be regarded as a complete analysis of the subjects discussed. All expressions of opinion are those of the author as of the date of publication and are subject to change. Content should not be construed as personalized investment advice nor should it be interpreted as an offer to buy or sell any securities mentioned. A financial advisor should be consulted before implementing any of the strategies presented.

Investing involves risk, including the potential loss of principal. No investment strategy can guarantee a profit or protect against loss in periods of declining values. Any references to protection benefits or guaranteed/lifetime income streams refer only to fixed insurance products, not securities or investment products. Insurance and annuity product guarantees are backed by the financial strength and claims-paying ability of the issuing insurance company.

Any names used in the examples in this book are hypothetical only and do not represent actual clients.

To everyone who has shown me there's more to life than paying bills and losing weight.

*Don't get so busy making a living
that you forget to make a life.*
~ Dolly Parton

Table of Contents

The Importance of Planning

Several times a year, my team and I host informational seminars and other events for soon-to-be retirees to help them plan retirement the right way. Often, attendees will visit my office later for a more personalized examination of their retirement prospects. Whenever I first sit down with such people, I encourage them to tell me what they *plan to do*, not what they *have done*. When people say what they *have done*, it almost never makes for a productive meeting. For example, about a year ago, I met with a couple who had attended one of my seminars two years earlier. They had retired to Arizona from the east coast to be closer to their kids. At first, they were confident in their nest egg. They had almost a million dollars in various assets, and they planned to grow that with strategic investment in real estate. Unfortunately, within two years, everything that could have gone wrong *did* go wrong.

When the husband first sat down across from me, he let out a heavy sigh and started with, "Let me tell you our story of woe." The story he went on to tell me was tragic but not unique. Sadly, I could almost predict every misstep before he explained it. Without any experience in real estate investment, they had made several losing investments. Eventually, they'd been forced to sell many properties at a loss. As of that day in my office, the couple was down $800,000, and things weren't looking up. I had to explain the reality of their situation: At least one of them would almost certainly have to go back to work.

They couldn't earn back enough money just from investments to sustain the quality of life to which they were accustomed throughout the entirety of their retirement.

The point of that story is not to instill fear. On the contrary, that couple's experience is an easily avoidable one. But the key is to consult with a professional before setting into motion any plans that may not achieve their intended purpose. That's why I can't stress it enough: Speak with a financial advisor when you're still planning what to do, not after you've already done something major. When people consider the biggest risks to a successful retirement, they often list things like market volatility or unexpected health problems. In fact, I believe that one of the biggest risks to retirement is failure to develop an effective plan. When prospective clients come to me with their "tales of woe," it almost always follows from neglecting to plan, or planning the wrong way. There are no do-overs in retirement. The margin for error is slim, and mistakes are not always fixable. That's why I've written this book: so you can plan *the right way.*

At my firm, we use a five-step proprietary process designed to help you retire as soon as possible, with confidence. The five steps cover:

1. Income
2. Investments
3. Tax efficiency
4. Health care and long-term care
5. Estate and legacy planning

The objective of this comprehensive plan is not just so you can get *to* retirement but to ensure you make it *through* retirement.

Sometimes people scoff at the idea of such rigorous planning. They tell me, "We need $3,000 a month to get by. All we want is to know if we'll have that." To be frank, I don't care about that. To me, retirement is not about the number you need to "get by;" it's about living your best life. It's not just to have what you need to cover the essentials but to have more so you can live comfortably and stress-free.

Money is the bottom line, but a fixed figure isn't planning for retirement. What happens when health care costs start rising? What about the constant risk of inflation? What about just the ability to make unnecessary purchases with confidence it will not derail your financial future? That's what a retirement plan should accomplish.

A financial planner's role is to answer the questions above, and more. They're also there to inspire confidence. Think about it; most people retire just once in their life. If they retire more times than that, it's probably because they made some serious mistakes. In contrast, my team helps hundreds of people retire every day! With that kind of experience, you can be sure, whatever comes your way, we're prepared to help you handle it.

Coupled with our experience is sophisticated software that can model almost every retirement eventuality. Knowing almost every potential hiccup that could potentially affect your retirement nest egg in advance is another powerful confidence builder. On their own, people often have some modicum of doubt when making the decision to retire. With an advisor, they can get around to living their lives with less worry about resources.

I want retirement to look like summer vacation at eight years old. Do you remember those days? Early in the morning, all the kids in the neighborhood would get together to play and hang out. At lunch you'd check in at home for a quick bite, but you couldn't wait to get back outside. You'd keep playing until dark when mom started calling for you. That was truly carefree living.

Retirement should be the same way. One of my client's told me he has a friend who spends every day in retirement watching the stock market. What kind of life is that? Unless market investment is genuinely your interest and hobby, that sounds terrible! I met another gentleman once who'd been retired for a year. I asked what he'd been doing, and he said he was figuring out Social Security . . . for an entire year! And he still hadn't figured it out. In half an hour, I told him everything he wanted to know and how to use it.

You know the expression, "Ready, aim, fire"? Those basic steps apply to retirement as well. Ready yourself as it approaches, aim for your goals with a well-made plan, and then fire—put it all into action. As a concept, it's very basic. But too often I see retirees "Ready, aim, aim, aim . . ." They never actually fire it because they're unsure of themselves, and they have too much to lose. People get so close to but never live the retirement they want. They think themselves out of taking action. You need to actually do it. Of course, you'll need a basis for confidence; I'm not encouraging you to behave recklessly. In this book, I'll outline the steps designed to help you retire confidently and achieving the life you've always envisioned. Keep reading for the complete guide on how to get more out of your retirement years!

CHAPTER 1

Longevity

You would think the prospect of the grave would loom more frightening as we age, yet many retirees say their number one fear is actually running out of money in their twilight years.[1] This fear is, unfortunately, justified, in part, because of one significant factor: We're living longer.

According to the Social Security Administration, in 1950, the average life expectancy for a sixty-five-year-old man was seventy-eight, and the average for a sixty-five-year-old woman was eighty-one. In 2020, those averages were eighty-three and eighty-eight, respectively.[2]

The bottom line of many retirees' budget woes comes down to this: They just didn't plan to live so long. Now, when we are young and in our working years, that's not something we necessarily see as a bad thing; don't some people fantasize about living forever, or at least reaching the ripe old age of one hundred?

Our resources are finite—we only have so much money to provide income—but our lifespans can be unpredictably long, perhaps longer than our resources allow. Also, longer lives

---

[1] Samiha Khanna. Journal of Accountancy. February 14, 2019. "Clients' Top Fear: Running out of Money."
https://www.journalofaccountancy.com/news/2019/feb/top-retirement-fears-201920387.html
[2] Social Security Administration. 2011 Trustees Report. "Actuarial Publications: Cohort Life Expectancy."
https://www.ssa.gov/OACT/TR/2011/lr5a4.html

don't necessarily equate with healthier lives. The longer you live, the more money you will likely need to spend on health care, even excluding long-term care needs like nursing homes.

You will also run into inflation. If you don't plan to live another twenty-five years but end up doing so, inflation at an average 2.5 percent will raise your $50,000-per-year budgeted need up to $93,000 per year. Or, if you live another eight years as inflation rises, you will need about $810,000 to cover those same expenses.[3] And this is before you count the expenses of any potential health care or long-term care needs.

Because we don't necessarily get to have our cake and eat it, too, our collective increased longevity hasn't necessarily increased the healthy years of our lives. Typically, our life-extending care most widely applies to the part of our lives where we will need more care in general. Think of a pacemaker at eighty-five, or radiation pills for cancer at seventy-eight.

"Wow, Chad," I can hear you say. "Way to start with the good news first."

I know, I've painted a fairly grim picture. But all I'm concerned about here is the cost. It's hard to put a dollar sign on life, but that is essentially what we're talking about when discussing longevity and your finances. According to the Stanford Center on Longevity, more than half of pre-retirees underestimate the life expectancy of the average sixty-five-year-old.[4] Living longer isn't a bad thing; it just costs more, and one key to a sound retirement strategy is preparing in advance for that expense.

One couple I know of illustrates this picture perfectly—I'll call them Joe and Jenny Winston. For most of their lives, Joe and Jenny were super aggressive investors, building a

---

3 Katie Brockman. The Motley Fool. August 19, 2018. "More Americans are Living into Their 90s—and That's Bad News for Their Savings."
https://www.fool.com/retirement/2018/08/19/more-americans-are-living-into-their-90s-and-thats.aspx
4 Stanford Center on Longevity. "Underestimating Years in Retirement."
http://longevity.stanford.edu/underestimating-years-in-retirement/

comfortable nest egg "just in case" health problems arose, they needed nursing home care, they had to move, or in case they needed to help children and grandchildren with their expenses. Having so many contingencies gave them personal confidence, as well as concretely increasing the likelihood that their plan would last over the long term. This is why we believe it is important to consider all areas of retirement.

Living longer may be more expensive, but it can be so meaningful when you plan for "what-ifs" and "just-in-cases."

Retiring Later

Planning for a long life in retirement partly comes down to when you retire. While many people end up retiring earlier than they anticipated—due to injuries, layoffs, family crises, and other unforeseen circumstances—continuing to work past age sixty (and even sixty-five) is still a viable option for others and can be an excellent way to help establish financial comfort in retirement.

There are many reasons for this. For one, you obviously still earn a paycheck and the benefits accompanying it. Medical coverage and beefing up your retirement accounts with further savings can be pretty significant by themselves, but the advantage of continuing your income is also that it should keep you from dipping into your retirement funds, further allowing them the opportunity to grow.

Additionally, for many workers, their nine-to-five job is more than just clocking in and out. Having a sense of purpose can keep us active physically, mentally, and socially. That kind of activity and level of engagement may also help stave off many of the health problems that affect retirees. Avoiding a sedentary life is one of the advantages of staying plugged into the workforce, if possible.

One example comes to mind of a guy who did just that. I first met him and his wife at one of my dinner seminars. Two weeks later they came to the office. The first thing the husband told me after sitting down at my desk was, "The day after your seminar, I quit my job." At first, I was panicked, thinking, "What in the world did I say?" But actually, this gentleman had already retired one time before. He'd gone back to work only because he was so bored in his retired life. Unfortunately, the new job he'd gotten was dreadful. He hated it. He knew financially he didn't have to be there, but making money is what he knew how to do. He took away from the seminar, though, that retirement is more than a money game.

It's not about working or not working—it's about finding enjoyment in what you do without having to stress over the money. This guy loved to work, but what he loved didn't pay as much as he could make elsewhere. Once he realized money didn't need to be his ultimate goal, he felt liberated. You'll probably never guess what work he found that he actually loved . . . Panning for gold. Talk about a unique interest! He and his buddies are bonafide gold hunting enthusiasts, and they're pretty good at it. It keeps them active, healthy, and happy.

Health Care

Take a second to reflect on your health care plan. Although working up to or even past age sixty-five would allow you to avoid a coverage gap between your working years and Medicare, that may not be an option for you. Even if it is, when you retire, you will need to make some decisions about what kind of insurance coverage you may need to supplement your Medicare. Are there any medical needs you have that may require coverage in addition to Medicare? Did your parents or grandparents have any inherited medical conditions you might consider using a special savings plan to cover?

These are all questions that are important to review with your financial professional so you can be sure you have enough money put aside for health care.

Long-Term Care

Longevity means the need for long-term care is statistically more likely to happen. If you intend to pass on a legacy, planning for long-term care is paramount, since it's estimated that nearly 70 percent of Americans will need some type of it.[5] However, this may be one of the biggest, most stressful pieces of longevity planning I encounter in my work. For one thing, who wants to talk about the point in their lives when they may feel the most limited? Who wants to dwell on what will happen if they no longer can toilet, bathe, dress, or feed themselves?

I get it; this is a less-than-fun part of planning. But a little bit of preparation now can go a long way!

When it comes to your longevity, just like with your goals, one of the important things to do is sit and dream. It may not be the fun, road-trip-to-the-Grand-Canyon kind of dreaming, but spend time envisioning how you want your twilight years to look.

For instance, if it is important for you to live in your home for as long as possible, who will provide for the day-to-day fixes and to-dos of housework if you become ill? Will you set aside money for a service, or do you have relatives or friends nearby whom you would comfortably allow to help you? Do you have a preference for in-home care over a nursing home or assisted living? This could be a good time to discuss the possibility of moving into a retirement community versus staying where you are or whether it's worth moving to another state and leaving relatives behind.

These are all important factors to discuss with your spouse and children, as *now* is the best time to address questions and concerns. For instance, is aging in place more important to one spouse than the other? Are the friends or relatives who live

---

5 Moll Law Group. 2019. "The Cost of Long-Term Care."
https://www.molllawgroup.com/the-cost-of-long-term-care.html

nearby emotionally, physically, and financially capable of helping you for a time if you face an illness?

Many families I meet with find these conversations very uncomfortable, particularly when children discuss nursing home care with their parents. A knee-jerk reaction for many is to promise they will care for their aging parents. This is noble and well-intentioned, but there needs to be an element of realism here. Does "help" from an adult child mean they stop by and help you with laundry, cooking, home maintenance, and bills? Or does it mean they move you into their spare room when you have hip surgery? Are they prepared to help you toilet and bathe if that becomes difficult for you to do on your own?

I don't mean to discourage families from caring for their own; this can be a profoundly admirable relationship when it works out. However, I've seen families put off planning for late-in-life care based on a tenuous promise the adult children would care for their parents, only to watch as the support system crumbles. Sometimes this is because the assumed caregiver hasn't given serious thought to the preparation they would need, both in a formal sense and with regard to their personal physical, emotional, and financial commitments. This is often also because we can't see the future: Alzheimer's and other maladies of old age can exact a heavy toll. When a loved one reaches the point he or she is at risk of wandering away or needs help with two or more activities of daily living, it can be more than one person or family can realistically handle.

If you know what you want, communicate with your family about both the best-case and worst-case scenarios. Then, hope for the best, and plan for the worst.

Realistic Cost of Care

Wrapped up in your planning should be a consideration for the cost of long-term care. Although the majority of us will need some degree of long-term care—including the 30 percent of us who may need up to five years of facility care—60 percent of us underestimate the costs of nursing home care! On average, consumers underestimate the annual cost of a private room in a nursing home by 51 percent.[6]

Another piece of long-term care costs is inflation.

It's common knowledge prices have been and keep rising, and that will lower your purchasing power on everything from food to medical care. Long-term care is a big piece of the inflation-disparity pie, which is part of why many find their estimates of nursing home care widely miss the mark. According to one survey, people expected to pay around $25,350 in out-of-pocket long-term care expenses per year, but, in reality, they'll more likely be paying over $47,000.[7]

While local costs vary from state to state, here's the national median for various forms of long-term care (plus projections that account for a 3 percent annual inflation, so you can see what I'm talking about):[8]

---

[6] Tamara E. Holmes. Yahoo Finance. July 24, 2019. "Consumers Underestimate Costs of Long-Term Care."
https://finance.yahoo.com/news/consumers-underestimate-costs-long-term-173542918.html

[7] Moll Law Group. 2019. "The Cost of Long-Term Care."
https://www.molllawgroup.com/the-cost-of-long-term-care.html

[8] Genworth Financial. May 2020. "Cost of Care Survey 2019."
https://www.genworth.com/aging-and-you/finances/cost-of-care.html

Long-Term Care Costs: Inflation				
	Home Health Care, Homemaker Services	Adult Day Care	Assisted Living	Nursing Home (semi-private)
Annual 2019	$51,480	$19,500	$48,612	$90,155
Annual 2029	$69,185	$26,206	$65,330	$121,161
Annual 2039	$92,979	$35,219	$87,799	$162,830
Annual 2049	$124,955	$47,332	$117,994	$218,830

Fund Your Long-Term Care

One critical mistake I see are those who haven't planned for long-term care because they assume the government will provide everything. But that's a huge misconception. The government has two health insurance programs: Medicare and Medicaid. These can greatly assist you in your health care needs in retirement but usually don't provide enough coverage to cover all of your health care costs in retirement. My firm isn't a government outpost, so we don't get to make decisions when it comes to forming policy and specifics about either one of these programs. I'm going to give the overview of both, but, if you want to dive into the details of these programs, you can visit Medicare.gov and Medicaid.gov.

Medicare

Medicare covers those aged sixty-five and older and those who are disabled. Medicare's coverage of any nursing-home-related health issues is limited. It might cover your nursing home stay if it is not a "custodial" stay, and it isn't long-term. For example, if you break a bone or suffer a stroke, stay in a nursing home for rehabilitative care, and then return home, Medicare may cover you. But, if you have developed dementia or are looking to move to a nursing facility because you can no longer bathe, dress, toilet, feed yourself, or take care of your hygiene, etc., then Medicare is not going to pay for your nursing home costs.[9]

Medicaid

Medicaid is a program the states administer, so funding, protocol, and limitations vary. Compared to Medicare, Medicaid more widely covers nursing home care, but it targets a different demographic than Medicare: those with low incomes.

If you have more assets than the Medicaid limit in your state and need nursing home care, you will need to use those assets to pay for your care. You will also have a list of additional state-approved ways to spend some of these assets over the Medicaid limit, such as pre-purchasing burial plots and funeral expenses or paying off debts. After that, your remaining assets fund your nursing home stay until they are gone, at which point Medicaid will jump in.

Some people aren't stymied by this, thinking they will just pass on their financial assets early, gifting them to relatives, friends, and causes so they can qualify for Medicaid when they need it. However, to prevent this exact scenario, Uncle Sam has implemented the look-back period. Currently, if you enroll in Medicaid, you are subject to having the government scrutinize the last five years of your finances for large gifts or expenses that may subject you to penalties, temporarily making you ineligible for Medicaid coverage.

---

9 Medicare.gov. "What Part A covers." https://www.medicare.gov/what-medicare-covers/part-a/what-part-a-covers.html

So, if you're planning to preserve your money for future generations and retain control of your financial resources during your lifetime, you'll probably want to prepare for the costs of longevity beyond a "government plan."

Self-Funding

One way to fund a longer life is the old-fashioned way, through self-funding. There are a variety of financial tools you can use, and they all have their pros and cons. If your assets are in low-interest accounts (savings, bonds, CDs), you risk letting inflation erode the value of your dollar. Or, if you are relying on the stock market, you have more growth potential, but you'll also want to consider the possible implications of market volatility. What if your assets take a hit? If you suffer a loss in your retirement portfolio in early or mid-retirement, you might have the option to "tighten your belt," so to speak, and cut back on discretionary spending to allow your portfolio the room to bounce back. But, if you are retired and depend on income from a stock account that just hit a downward stride, what are you going to do?

HSAs

These days, you might also be able to self-fund through a health savings account, or HSA, if you have access to one through a high-deductible health plan (you will not qualify to save in an HSA after enrolling in Medicare). In an HSA, any growth of your tax-deductible contributions will be tax-free, and any distributions paid out for qualified health costs are also tax-free. That can be a tax trifecta. Long-term care expenses count as health costs, so, if this is an option available to you, it is one way to use the tax advantages to self-fund your longevity. Bear in mind, if you are younger than sixty-five, any money you use for nonqualified expenses will be subject to taxes and penalties, and, if you are older than sixty-five, any HSA money you use for non-medical expenses is subject to income tax.

LTCI

One slightly more nuanced way to pay for longevity, specifically for long-term care, is long-term care insurance, or LTCI. As car insurance protects your assets in case of a car accident and home insurance protects your assets in case something happens to your house, long-term care insurance aims to protect your assets in case you need long-term care in an at-home or nursing home situation.

As with other types of insurance, you will pay a monthly premium in exchange for an insurance company to pay for long-term care down the road. Typically, policies cover two to three years of care, which is adequate for an "average" situation: it's estimated 70 percent of Americans will need about three years of long-term care of some kind. However, it's important to consider you might not be "average" when you are preparing for long-term care costs; on average, 20 percent of today's sixty-five-year-olds will need care for longer than five years. [10]

Now, there are a few oft-cited components of LTCI that make it unattractive for some:

- Expense — LTCI can be expensive. It is generally less expensive the younger you are, but a fifty-five-year-old couple who purchased LTCI in 2019 could expect to pay $3,050 each year for an average three-year coverage policy. And the annual cost only increases from there the older you are. [11]

- Limited options — Let's face it: LTCI is expensive for consumers, but it is also expensive for companies that offer it. With fewer companies willing to take on that

---

[10] David Levine. *U.S. News.* July 10, 2019. "How to Pay for Nursing home Costs." https://health.usnews.com/best-nursing-homes/articles/how-to-pay-for-nursing-home-costs

[11] American Association for Long-Term Care Insurance. January 2019. "2019 National Long-Term Care Insurance Price Index." https://www.aaltci.org/news/wp-content/uploads/2019/01/2019-Price-Index-LTC.pdf

expense, this narrows the market, meaning opportunities to price shop for policies with different options or custom benefits are limited.

- If you know you need it, you may not be able to get it — Insurance companies offering LTCI are taking on a risk that you may need LTCI. That risk is the foundation of the product—you may or may not need it. If you know you will need it because you have a dementia diagnosis or another illness for which you will need long-term care, you will likely not qualify for LTCI coverage.
- Use it or lose it — If you have LTCI and are in the minority of Americans who die having never needed long-term care, all the money you paid into your LTCI plan is gone.
- Possibly fluctuating rates — Your premium rate is not locked in on LTCI. Companies maintain the ability to raise or lower your premium amounts. This means some seniors face an ultimatum: Keep funding a policy at what might be a less affordable rate *or* lose coverage and let go of all the money they paid in thus far.

After that, you might be thinking, "How can people possibly be interested in LTCI?" But let me repeat myself—as many as 70 percent of Americans will need long-term care. Those are pretty steady odds. And, although only 8 percent of Americans have purchased LTCI, keep in mind the costs of nursing home care. Can you afford $7,000 a month to put into nursing home care and still have enough left over to protect your legacy? This is a very real concern: One study says 72 percent of Americans are impoverished by the end of just one year in a nursing home.[12] So, not to sound like a broken record, but it is vitally important to have a plan in place to deal with longevity and long-term care if you intend to leave a financial legacy.

---

[12] A Place for Mom. January 2018. "Long-Term Care Insurance: Costs & Benefits." http://www.aplaceformom.com/senior-care-resources/articles/long-term-care-costs.

Long-term care insurance is kind of a black cloud that hangs over many retirees because they don't know how to plan for it. The costs are high, there are a limited number of companies that even offer it anymore, and there are stories of people who were priced out right before they needed it. With couples, especially, there is a significant chance at least one of the spouses may not ultimately take advantage of long-term care facilities anyway. So, the end result? They give away thousands in premiums to an insurance company and receive nothing in return.

In an effective retirement plan, we try to address each of the issues that may arise in retirement—the market declining, health issues arising, etc.—and allot funds accordingly. As for health care expenses, one option is to self-insure. Many of my clients are actually very capable of doing that. At first they may worry about the price of a memory care unit, but that's before really examining their assets. They may have income from Social Security, a $400,000 house with no mortgage, and a small pension. If they need long-term care, those assets would more than likely cover the expense.

Another option I find often works nicely for many retirees is to use add an optional rider on their annuity or life insurance policy. Long-term care riders can serve almost as a guarantee. Still, it's not the end-all. If you sit down with a long-term care insurance salesman, he or she might make it sound like a rider is essential for everyone. That's not entirely true, but it may be a good choice for your circumstances. Just remember this, there are always other options.

Product Riders

Some companies are getting creative with their products, particularly insurance companies. One way they are retooling to meet people's needs is through optional product riders on annuities and life insurance. Elsewhere in this book, I talk about annuity basics, and here's a brief overview: Annuities are insurance contracts. You pay the insurance company a premium, either as a lump sum or as a series of payments over a set amount of time, in exchange for guaranteed income payments. One of the advantages of an annuity is it has access to riders, which allow you to tweak your contract for a fee, usually about 1 percent of the contract value annually. One annuity rider some companies offer is a long-term care rider. If you have an annuity with a long-term care rider and are not in need of long-term care, your contract behaves as any annuity contract would—nothing changes. Generally speaking, if you reach a point when you can't perform multiple functions of daily life on your own, you notify the insurance company, and a representative will turn on those provisions of your contract.

Like LTCI, different companies and products offer different options. Some annuity long-term care riders offer coverage of two years in a nursing home situation. Others cap expenses at two times the original annuity's value. It greatly depends. Some people prefer this option because there isn't a "use-it-or-lose-it" piece; if you die without ever having needed long-term care, you still will have had the income benefit from the base contract. Still, as with any annuities or insurance contracts, there are the usual restrictions and limitations. Withdrawing money from the contract will affect future income payments, early distributions can result in a penalty, income taxes may apply, and, because the insurance company's solvency is what guarantees your payments, it's important to do your research about the insurance company you are considering purchasing a contract from.

Understandably, a discussion on long-term care and its particulars is bound to feel at least a little tedious. Yet, this is a critical piece of planning for income in retirement, particularly if you want to leave a legacy.

I met a couple once who had waited until the time when they needed money for long-term care to start planning for it. So, when's the best time to get LTCI if you want it? *When you don't need it.* The most common situation I see is clients coming to us about their parents. Their parents need to go into a care facility, and the kids don't know how to pay for it. They come to me and ask if they can get LTCI or something like it. If that's your situation, I'm sorry to say it, but, no, you probably can't get LTCI at that point. And, even if you can, it's more than likely going to be astronomically expensive.

Remember though, LTCI isn't the only option. I think of it like owning a tow truck. If your car ever breaks down, it'd be convenient to own your own tow truck. But many people will never in their lives require a tow. So, what would be the value of owning a tow truck?

LTCI is the same way. It can be nice to have if you really need it, but many won't ever capitalize on its value. If you don't feel like "owning the tow truck," there are other alternatives available to you.

Spousal Planning

Here's one thing to keep in mind no matter how you plan to save: Many of us will be planning for more than ourselves. Look back at all the stats on health events and the likelihood of long life and long-term care. If they hold true for a single individual, then the likelihood of having a costly health or long-term care event is even higher for a married couple. You'll be planning for not just one life but two. So, when it comes to long-term care insurance, annuities, self-funding, or whatever strategy you are looking at utilizing, be sure you are funding longevity for the both of you.

When you're married, long-term care planning can get complicated. It's not as simple as accounting for just your own life expectancy. It's about yours *and* your spouse's, and it's a challenge to account for two unknown variables instead of just one. All your decisions must be interwoven. You need to know things like, what's the spousal benefit on your pension?

I'm always shocked by how many people don't know the answer to that question. They know they're getting monthly income from their pension but not how much goes to their spouse if they die. It could carry over entirely, plus your Social Security. On the other hand, such assets could disappear almost entirely after your death. Then what is your spouse to do?

Such questions need to be asked long before the answers become relevant. That's part of what a financial advisor is designed to do—to ask the tough questions you don't want to think about or you might not consider until it's too late. The moral of the story is this: Know the details, and plan accordingly early in the retirement process.

CHAPTER 2

Taxes

Where to begin with taxes? Perhaps by acknowledging we all bear responsibility for the resources we share. Roads, bridges, schools . . . It is the patriotic duty of every American to pay their fair share of taxes. Many would agree with me, though, while they don't mind paying their fair share, they're not interested in paying one cent more!

Now, just talking taxes probably takes your mind to April—tax season. You are probably thinking about all the forms you collect and how you file. Perhaps you are thinking about your certified public accountant or another qualified tax professional and saying to yourself, "I've already got taxes taken care of, thanks!"

However, what I see when people come into my office is that their relationship with their tax professional is purely a January through April relationship. That means they may have a tax professional but not a tax *planner*.

What I mean is tax planning extends beyond filing taxes. In April, we are required to settle our accounts with the IRS to make sure we have paid up on our bill or to even the score if we have overpaid. But real tax planning is about making each financial move in a way that allows you to keep the most money in your pocket and out of Uncle Sam's.

Now, as a caveat, I want to emphasize I am neither a CPA nor a tax planner, but I see the way taxes affect my clients, and I have plenty of experience helping clients implement tax-efficient strategies in their retirement plans—in conjunction with their tax professionals.

To cover the details that do require a CPA, my office has a strategic partnership with an accounting firm. They specialize in trust work, working predominantly with individuals, families, and small business, which is not, by the way, what all CPAs necessarily do. Our partner shares our same views about the future of taxes, how Roth IRAs can be implemented, and the care that needs to be taken with taxes on Medicare premiums. Those are all important details that, unfortunately, not all CPAs are well versed in.

We're also happy our partner gives complimentary consultations just like we do, something that has become uncommon in the field these days. We talk often to discuss client strategies and how we might optimize their tax efficiency. Representatives from their office also join us for client events and seminars a few times a year. I have asked all my clients for feedback on their experience with our recommended CPA, and I've heard nothing but positive reviews.

It is especially important to me to help my clients develop tax-efficient strategies in their retirement plans because each dollar they can keep in their pockets is a dollar we can put to work.

We met a couple about a year ago, at the end of the year. They did not qualify for Medicare yet, so they were on the Affordable Care Act plan, receiving a subsidy from the government. At the end of each fiscal year, their finance guy (a broker) would make a series of adjustments in a trust account they owned to increase gains. To them, that was exactly what they wanted. It earned them a few extra thousand dollars per year. But, that extra bit of income was taxable and just large enough to push them beyond the income threshold that disqualified them for their government subsidy. In effect, they sacrificed about $12,000 in subsidy funds to earn a couple thousand dollars in added income. How much sense does that make? None, in my mind.

With regular taxes, it's not the end of the world if you slip into a higher tax bracket. After all, you only pay more in taxes on that extra bit of money. But, with Medicare expenses and health care subsidies, passing the threshold even by a dollar is enough to disqualify you. You stand to lose thousands just to gain a dollar. Decisions like that involve taxation, but not all tax professionals know to account for it.

Another client of mine is actually a CPA. I was confused when he first came to me looking for a retirement plan and a secondary opinion. When I asked why, he said it was because he'd made a big Roth conversion a couple years earlier, failed to account for all facets of retirement planning, and, thus, had overlooked the fact his conversion would increase his Medicare premium significantly. He wanted to work with us because, even though he knew taxes, he didn't understand *complete* retirement planning. Knowing taxes by themselves is not always good enough. One needs to understand every aspect of retirement and how each piece—taxes included—figures into a larger plan.

The Fed

Now, in the United States, taxes can be a rather uncertain proposition. Depending on who is in the White House and which party controls Congress, we might be tempted to assume tax rates could either decline or increase in the next four to eight years accordingly. However, there is one (large!) factor we, as a nation, must confront: the national debt.

Currently, according to USDebtClock.org, we are over $25,000,000,000,000 in debt and climbing. That's $25 TRILLION with a "T." With just $1 trillion, you could park it in the bank at a zero percent interest rate and still spend more than $54 million every day for fifty years without hitting a zero balance.

Even if Congress got a handle and stopped that debt from its daily compound, divided by each taxpayer, we each would owe about $175,000. So, will that be check or cash?

My point here isn't to give you anxiety. I'm just saying, even with the rosiest of outlooks on our personal income tax rates, you cannot count on low tax rates for the long term. Instead, you and your network of professionals (tax, legal, and financial) should constantly be looking for ways to take advantage of tax-saving opportunities as they come. After all, the best "luck" is when proper planning meets opportunity.

So, how can we get started?

Know Your Limits

One of the foundational pieces of tax planning is knowing what tax bracket you are in based on your income after subtracting pre-tax or untaxed assets. Your income taxes are based on is everything on which you have to pay taxes.

One reason to know your income tax rate is so you can see how far away you are from the next lower or higher tax bracket. This is particularly important when it comes to decisions, such as gifting and Roth IRA rollovers.

For instance, based on the 2020 tax table, Mallory and Ralph's taxable income was just over $330,000, putting them in the 32 percent tax bracket and $3,400 above the upper end of the 24 percent tax bracket. They already maxed out their retirement funds' tax-exempt contributions for the year. Their daughter, Gloria, was a sophomore in college. This couple could shave a considerable amount off their tax bill if they use the $3,400 to help Gloria out with groceries and school—something they were likely to do, anyway, but now can deliberately put to work for them in their overall financial strategy.

Now, I use Mallory and Ralph only as an example—your circumstances may be different—but I think this nicely illustrates the way planning ahead for taxes can save you money.

Assuming a Lower Tax Rate

Many people anticipate being in a lower tax bracket in retirement. It makes sense: You won't be contributing to retirement funds; you'll be drawing from them. And you won't have all those work expenses—work clothes, transportation, etc.

Yet, do you really plan on changing your lifestyle after retirement? Do you plan to cut down on the number of times you eat out, scale back vacations, and skimp on travel?

What I see in my office is many couples spend more in the first few years, or maybe the first decade, of retirement. Sure, later on, that may taper off, but usually only just in time for their budget to be eaten up in health and long-term care expenses. Do you see where this is going? Many people plan as though their taxable income will be lower in retirement and are surprised when the tax bills come in and look more or less the same as they used to. It's better to plan for the worst and hope for the best, wouldn't you agree?

401(k)/IRA

One sometimes unexpected piece of tax planning in retirement concerns your 401(k) or IRA. Most of us have one of these accounts or an equivalent. Throughout our working lives, we pay in, dutifully socking away a portion of our earnings in these tax-deferred accounts. There's the rub: tax-deferred. Not tax-free. Very rarely is anything free of taxation when you get down to it. Using 401(k)s and IRAs in retirement is no different. The taxes the government deferred when you were in your working years are now coming due, and you will pay taxes on that income at whatever your current tax rate is.

Just to ensure Uncle Sam gets his due, the government also has a required minimum distribution, or RMD, rule. Beginning at age seventy-two, you are required to withdraw a certain minimum amount every year from your 401(k) or IRA, or else you will face a 50 percent tax penalty on any RMD monies you should have withdrawn but didn't—and that's on top of income tax.

Of course, there is also the Roth account. You can think of the difference between a Roth and a traditional retirement account as the difference between taxing the seed and taxing the harvest. Because Roths pay taxes on the front end, there aren't tax penalties for early withdrawals of the principal nor are there taxes on the growth after you reach age fifty-nine-and-one-half. Perhaps best of all, there are no RMDs. Of course, you must own a Roth account for a minimum of five years before you are able to take advantage of all of its features.

This is one more area where it pays to be aware of your tax bracket. Some people may find it advantageous to "convert" their traditional retirement account funds to Roth account funds in a year they are in a lower tax bracket. Others may opt to put any excess RMDs from their traditional retirement accounts into other products, like stocks or insurance. *A Roth Conversion is a taxable event and may have several tax related consequences. Be sure to consult with a qualified tax advisor before making any decisions regarding your IRA.*

Does that make your head spin? Understandable. That's why it's so important to work with a financial professional and tax planner who can help you not only execute these sorts of tax-efficient strategies but also help you understand what you are doing and why.

Tax efficiency is the most popular seminar my firm hosts. Social Security and Medicare aren't going away entirely, as some would suggest, but eventually the mounting bill has got to get paid. The IRS and federal government make the rules for how that happens.

I believe that means taxes will go up, especially on things like IRAs and 401(k)s. People are often led to believe taxes are inevitable and fixed—that one can't do anything about it. But that's not true. We can't establish the rules, but we can use them to our advantage.

One big myth I hear often is that you should put money into an IRA because the money grows "faster." That's just not true, though. People forget the money in their traditional IRAs does not all belong to them, you still owe taxes at some point. If it's in a Roth, on the other hand, it's all yours. Saying you're a millionaire because a million dollars is in your traditional IRA is like saying you own your house even though there's twenty years left on your mortgage. Make sure you have a comprehensive tax plan in place to ensure you don't give up money to Uncle Sam to which he's not entitled.

CHAPTER 3

Market Volatility

Up and down. Roller coaster. Merry-go-round. Bulls and bears. Peak-to-trough.

Sound familiar? This is the language we use to talk about the stock market. With volatility and spikes, even our language is jarring, bracing, and vivid.

Still, financial strategies tend to revolve around market-based products, for good reasons. For one thing, there is no other financial class that packs the same potential for growth, pound for pound, as stock-based products. Because of growth potential, inflation protection, and new opportunities, it may be unwise to avoid the market entirely.

However, along with the potential for growth is the potential for loss. Many of the people I see in my office come in still feeling a bit burned from the market drama of 2000 to 2010. That was a rough stretch, and many of us are once-bitten-twice-shy investors, right?

So how do we balance these factors? How do we try to satisfy both the need for protection and the need for growth?

For one thing, it is important to recognize the value of diversity. Now, I'm not just talking about the diversity of assets among different kinds of stocks, or even different kinds of stocks and bonds. That's only one kind of diversity; while important, both stocks and bonds, though different, are still market-based products. Just as an incoming tide raises all boats, most market-based products tend to rise or lower as a whole, so diversity among stocks and bonds won't protect your assets during times when the market as a whole is in decline. Therefore, a portfolio diverse in only market-sourced products won't automatically protect your assets during times when the market declines.

In addition to the sort of "horizontal diversity" you have by purchasing a variety of stocks and bonds from different companies, I encourage having "vertical diversity," or diversity among asset classes. This means having different product types, including both securities products and insurance products—with varying levels of growth potential, liquidity, and protection—all in accordance with your unique situation, goals, and needs.

Many financial professionals assess risk tolerance simply using a person's age and investment types. I understand the value in knowing those variables, but it's hardly the whole picture. That kind of risk assessment assumes every person of the same age should invest the same way or that risk management can work around one's propensity for aggressive or conservative investment style. In fact, investment style is often one of the first and most significant things that needs to change as we age. But each person is different. If you want a recommendation of how to assess your risk, it involves more than some basic data.

Many years ago, a family member had some health troubles. She visited a doctor for help, and the doctor gave her three options to consider. Her response was, "That's great. So which do you recommend?" He didn't want to answer. I'm sure he had his reasons, but his response was frustrating to us. We didn't want just a list of options; we were there for medical advice based on his experience and insight.

In the same way, it's not enough to plug some information into a computer, print out a "risk assessment," and list a series of options. You can find options on your own by reading a book like this one. What you want is a professional's recommendation. For financial advisors to make an educated recommendation, they need to know more than your age and investment portfolio. They should be asking what you need your money to do and when you need it to do those things. Those are the crucial factors in evaluating risk and making financial recommendations.

At my office, we take a bucket approach to money. We evaluate income needs individually: what it's for, where it comes from, and when you'll need it—not just from your perspective now but from years down the line, even after potential life changes.

The Color of Money

When you're looking at your overall portfolio diversity, part of the equation is knowing which products fit into which category: what has liquidity, what has protection, and what has growth potential.

Before we dive in, keep in mind these aren't absolutes. You might think of liquidity, growth, and protection as primary colors. While some products will look pretty much yellow, red, or blue, others will have a mix of characteristics, making them more green, orange, or purple.

Growth

I like to think of the growth category as red. It's powerful, it's somewhat volatile, and it's also the category where we have the greatest opportunity for growth and loss. Often, products in the growth category will have a good deal of liquidity but very little protection. These are our market-based products and strategies, and we think of them mostly in shades of red and orange, to designate their growth and liquidity. This is a good place to be when you're young—think fast cars and flashy leather jackets—but its allure often wanes as you move closer to retirement. Examples of "red" products include:

- Stocks
- Equities
- Exchange-traded funds
- Mutual funds
- Corporate bonds
- Real estate investment trusts
- Speculations
- Alternative investments

Liquidity

Yellow is my liquidity category color. I typically recommend having at least enough yellow money to cover six months' to a year's worth of expenses in case of emergency. Yellow assets don't need a lot of growth potential; they just need to be readily available when we need them. The "yellow" category includes:

- Cash
- Money market accounts

Protection

The color of protection, to me, is blue. Tranquil, peaceful, sure, even if it lacks a certain amount of flash. This is the direction I like to see people move toward as they're nearing retirement. The red, flashy look of stock market returns and the risk of possible overnight losses is less attractive as we near retirement and look for more consistency and reliability. While this category doesn't come with a lot of liquidity, the products here are backed by an insurance company, a bank, or a government entity. "Blue" products include:

- Certificates of deposit – which are FDIC insured

- Government-based bonds – which are backed by the US Government
- Life insurance- backed by the financial strength of the issuing company
- Annuities- backed by the financial strength of the issuing company

I typically advise my clients to allocate their portfolio among all three categories, as their circumstances and risk tolerance allows. Some of their money should be housed in "safer" options and some in market investments.

If you're not happy making 1 or 2 percent, there are often really only two things you can do. One: You can invest in the stock market. Two: You can sacrifice some liquidity. In the latter option, you can choose CDs, which will earn maybe 3 percent at the highest. Personally, I'm not a big fan of CDs for a large portion of one's assets. If the market has 20 percent growth for a time, you've missed out on a lot of potential earnings. On the other hand, things like CDs offer a measure of protection you can't expect from the market. The key is balance.

401(k)s

I want to take a second to specifically address a product many retirees will be using to build their retirement income: the 401(k) and other retirement accounts. Any of these retirement accounts (IRAs, 401(k)s, 403(b)s, etc.) are basically "tax wrappers." What do I mean by that? Well, depending on your plan provider, a 401(k) could include target-date funds, passively managed products, stocks, bonds, mutual funds, or even variable, fixed and fixed index annuities, all collected in one place and governed by rules (aka the "tax wrapper"). These rules govern how much money you can put inside, what ways you can put it in, when you will pay taxes on it, and when you can take the money out. Inside the 401(k), each of the products inside the "tax wrapper" might have its own fees or commissions, in addition to the management fee you pay on the 401(k) itself.

Now, fees can be troublesome. You can't get something for nothing, and fees are how many financial companies and professionals make a living. Yet, it's important to recognize even a fee of a single percentage point is money out of your pocket—money that represents not just the one-time fee of today but also represents an opportunity cost. One study found a single percentage fee could cost a millennial close to $600,000 in his or her lifetime.[13] For someone closer to retirement, how much do you think fees may have cost?

Even for those close to retirement, it's important to look at management fees and assess if you think you're getting what you pay for. Over the course of ten years, those puppies can add up, and you may have decades ahead of you in which you will need to rely on your assets.

Dollar-Cost Averaging

With 401(k) and other market-based retirement products (IRAs, 403(b)s, etc.), when you are investing for the long term, the concept of dollar-cost averaging works in your favor. When the market is trending up, if you are consistently paying in money, month over month, great; your investments are growing, and you are adding to your assets. When the market takes a dip, no problem; your dollars buy more shares at a lower price. At some point, the market will likely rebound, in which case your shares might increase and possibly be more valuable than they were before. This phenomenon is what we call dollar-cost averaging. It doesn't guarantee a profit or that you can't

---

[13] Dayana Yochim and Jonathan Todd. NerdWallet. "How a 1% Fee Could Cost Millennials $590,000 in Retirement Savings." https://www.nerdwallet.com/blog/investing/millennial-retirement-fees-one-percent-half-million-savings-impact/

lose money in a declining market, but it's a smart strategy to help smooth out market volatility in your portfolio.

However, when you are in retirement, this strategy may work against you. You may even hear of the term "reverse" dollar-cost averaging. Before, when the market lost ground, you were bargain-shopping; your dollars purchased more assets at a reduced price. When you are in retirement, you are no longer the purchaser; you are selling. So, in a down market, you have to sell more assets to make the same amount of money as what you did in a favorable market.

I've had lots of people step into my office to talk to me about this, emphasizing, "My advisor says the market always bounces back, and I just have to hold on for the long term."

There's truth in that. Thus far, the market has always rebounded to higher heights than before. But the prospect of potentially higher returns in five years may not be very helpful in retirement if you are relying on the income from those returns, for example, to pay this month's electric bill.

Building a plan with a bucket approach to firmly establish risk tolerance helps ensure you're not caught off-guard when the market dips. Over time, usually every six to twelve months, your plan must be updated and a little money shifted between buckets to account for your ever-changing risk tolerance.

Is There a "Perfect" Product?

To bring us back around to the discussion of protection, growth, and liquidity, the ideal product would be a "ten" in all three categories, right? Completely guaranteed, doubling in size every few years, and accessible whenever you want. Does such a product exist? Anyone who says, "yes" is either ignorant or malevolent.

Instead of running in circles looking for that perfect product—the silver bullet, the unicorn of financial strategies—

it's more important to circle back to the concept of a balanced, asset-diverse portfolio.

This is why your interests may be best served when you work with a trusted financial professional who knows what various financial products can do and how you can use them in your personal retirement plan.

We believe to help combat inflation, for most people, at least some money needs to stay in the market. In part, the market is designed to help investors account for inflation. But again, balance is key. Some of my clients want to put all their money into "safe" options. In the long run, however, that will likely lose them money because of the loss of purchasing power.

A 3 percent return when the inflation rate is also 3 percent really only means your money is stagnant—its value is constant due to the devaluing effect of inflation. Inflation is a big issue and one that's under-appreciated by many soon-to-be retirees. You shouldn't count the stock market out entirely but neither should it be your primary investment avenue.

CHAPTER 4

Retirement Income

Retirement. For many of us, it's what we've saved for and dreamed of, pinning our hopes to a magical someday. Is that someday full of traveling? Is it filled with grandkids? Gardening? Maybe your fondest dream is just never having to work again, never having to clock in or be accountable to someone else.

Your ability to do these things all hinges on *income*. Without the money to support these dreams, even a basic level of work-free lifestyle is unsustainable. That's why planning for your income in retirement is so foundational. But where do we begin?

It can be easy to feel overwhelmed by this question. Some may feel the urge to amass a large lump sum and then try to put it all in one product—insurance, investments, liquid assets—to provide all the growth, liquidity, and income they need. Instead, I think you need a more balanced approach. After all, retirement planning isn't magic. There is no single product that can be all things to all people (or even all things to one person), and no approach works unilaterally for everyone. That's why it's important to talk to a financial professional who can help you lay down the basics and take you step by step through the planning process. Not only will you have the assurance you have addressed the areas you need to, but you will also have an ally who can help you break the process down and help keep you from feeling overwhelmed.

Sources of Income

Thinking of all the pieces of your retirement expenses might be intimidating. But, like cleaning out a junk drawer or revisiting that garage remodel, once you have laid everything out, you can begin to arrange things into categories.

Once you have a good overall picture of where your expenses will lie, you can start stacking up the resources to cover them.

Social Security

Social Security is a guaranteed, inflation-protected federal insurance program playing a significant part in most of our retirement plans. From delaying until you've reached full retirement age or beyond to examining spousal benefits, as I discuss elsewhere in this book, there is plenty you can do to try to make the most of this monthly benefit. As with all of your retirement income sources, it's important to see how to make this resource stretch to provide the most bang and buck for your situation.

Pension

Another generally reliable source of retirement income for you might be a pension, if you are one of the lucky people who still have them.

If you don't have a pension, go ahead and skim on down to the next point, but, if you do have a pension, let's take a second to take a closer look.

Because your pension can be such a central piece of your retirement income plan, you will want to put some thought into answering basic questions about it.

How well is your pension funded? Since the heyday of the pension, companies and governments have neglected to fund their pension obligations, creating a persistent problem with this otherwise reliable asset. A report by the American Legislative Exchange Council revealed a $5.96 trillion deficit in state pension funds overall in 2018.[14] Is your pension one of those?

In addition to checking up on your pension's health, check into what your options are for taking your pension. If you have already retired and made those decisions, this may be a foregone conclusion. If not, it pays to know what you can expect and what decisions you can make, such as taking spousal options to cover your husband or wife if he or she outlives you.

Also, some companies are incentivizing lump-sum payouts of pensions to reduce the companies' payment liabilities. If that's the case with your employer, talk to your financial professional to see if it might be prudent to do something like that or if it might be better to stick with lifetime payments or other options.

Your 401(k) and IRA

The "modern way" to save for retirement is in a 401(k) or IRA (or their nonprofit and governmental equivalents). These tax-advantaged accounts are, overall, a poor substitute for pensions, but one of the biggest disservices we do to ourselves is to not take full advantage of them in the first place. According to one article, about 42 percent of adults under thirty and 26 percent of adults thirty to forty-four haven't contributed to any retirement account, let alone their 401(k). [15]

---

[14] Jonathan Williams, Christine Smith, Thurston Powers, and Bob Williams. ALEC. March 20, 2019. "Unaccountable and Unaffordable 2018." https://www.alec.org/publication/unaccountable-and-unaffordable-2018/

[15] Niall McCarthy. Forbes. June 3, 2019. "Report: A Quarter of Americans Have No Retirement Savings." https://www.forbes.com/sites/niallmccarthy/2019/06/03/report-a-

Also, if you have changed jobs over the years, do the work of tracking down any benefits from your past employers. You might have an IRA here or a 401(k) there; keep track of those so you can pull them together and look at those assets when you're ready to begin establishing sources of retirement income.

Other Assets

- Do you have life insurance?
- Do you have any annuities?
- How about long-term care insurance?
- Any passive income sources?
- Stock and bond portfolios?
- Liquid assets? (What's in your bank account?)
- Any alternative investments?
- How about rental properties?

It's important, if you are going through the work of sitting with a financial professional, to look at your retirement income picture and pull together *all* of your assets, no matter how big or small. From the free insurance policy offered at your bank to the sizeable investment in your brother-in-law's modestly successful furniture store, you want to have a good idea of where your money is.

Every week, I sit down with people who underestimate how much money they have. In turn, they underestimate their ability to retire. In my first meeting with new clients, I ask them to bring in documentation of all their assets and investments. My team then evaluates this data in the next few days, and we compile a report to share with clients during their second meeting. We find that some clients are right where they thought, and others are way off. This is one reason why we feel

---

quarter-of-americans-have-no-retirement-savings-infographic/#5fb35b703ebf

it is important to seek advice from a financial advisor. If you're unsure where your finances are, we can help.

Retirement Income Needs

How much income will you need in retirement? How do you determine that? A lot of people work toward a random number, thinking, "If I can just have a million dollars, I'll be comfortable in retirement!" Don't get me wrong; it is possible to save up a lot of money and then retire in the hopes you can keep your monthly expenses lower than some set estimation. But I think this carries a general risk of running out of money. Instead, I work with my clients to find out what their current and projected income needs are and then work from there to see how we might cover any gaps between what they have and what they want.

Goals and Dreams

I like to start with your pie in the sky. Do you find yourself planning for your vacations more thoroughly than you do your retirement? A recent survey found one in five Americans spend more time planning our vacations than we spend planning our retirements.[16] Maybe it's because planning a vacation is less stressful: Having a week at the beach go awry is, well, a walk on the beach compared to running out of money in retirement. Whatever the case, perhaps it would be better if you thought of your retirement as a vacation in and of itself—no clocking in, no boss, no overtime. If you felt unlimited by financial strain, what would you do?

---

[16] Malika Mitra. CNBC. August 2, 2019. "You're not alone if you spend more time planning your vactation than working on your finances." https://www.cnbc.com/2019/08/02/1-in-5-people-spend-more-time-planning-vacations-than-finances-survey.html

Would an endless vacation for you mean Paris and Rome? Would it mean mentoring at children's clubs or serving at the local soup kitchen? Or maybe it would mean deepening your ties to those immediately around you—neighbors, friends, and family. Maybe it would mean more time to enjoy hobbies and activities you love. Have you been considering a second (or even third) act as a small business owner, turning a hobby or passion into a revenue source?

This is your time to daydream and answer the question: If you could do anything, what would you do?

After that, it's just a matter of putting a dollar amount on it. What are the costs of round-the-world travel? One couple I know said their highest priority in retirement was being able to take each of their grandchildren on a cross-country vacation every year. That's a pretty specific goal—one that is reasonably easy to nail down a budget for.

One woman who came into my office said all she ever wanted was a cute little convertible car. That was her life's dream. She had never felt the kind of confidence in her finances to feel comfortable owning this car, but having this specific objective in mind is something that can make planning the monetary side of retirement much easier.

Current Budget

A current expense report is one of the trickiest pieces of retirement spending. Most people assume the expenses of their lives in retirement will be different—lower. After all, there will be no drive to work, no need to keep a formal wardrobe, and, perhaps most impactful of all, no more saving for retirement!

Yet, we often underestimate our daily spending habits. That's why I typically ask my clients to bring in their bank statements for the past year—they are reflective of your *actual* spending, not just what you think you're spending.

A lot of people haven't lived on a budget for many years, but it's essential to have a budget in retirement. In their first couple meetings, I'll offer new clients some worksheets we use to help people evaluate their assets and income. We also provide forms to breakdown what potential expenses they may have in years to come. Finally, we tend to add a buffer on top of their estimation, just to be careful. From all that information, we can identify pretty closely how much money clients will need to live confidently.

I also point out to people how they will likely spend more in retirement than they did in their working years—at least at the beginning. Retirement is like a week full of Saturdays. I don't know about you, but I spend more money on Saturday, when I have time to do what I want, than during the week when I'm busy at work. Every day is like that once you've stopped working. Once people account for that change in their circumstances, they're likely better prepared to correctly estimate their spending trend for the next several years.

I can't count the number of times I have sat with a couple, asked them about their spending, and had them throw out a number that seemed incredibly low. When I ask them where the number came from, they usually say they estimated based off of their total bills. Yet, our spending is so much more than our mortgage, utilities, cable, phone, car, grocery, or credit card bills.

"What about clothes?" I ask, "Or dining out? What about gifts and coffees and last-minute birthday cards?" That's when the lights come on.

This is why I suggest collecting a year's worth of information. There is usually no such thing as a one-time purchase. Did you buy new furniture? Even if that is a rarity, do you think that will be the last time you *ever* buy furniture?

On the other hand, some people overestimate their expenses, and they're happily surprised to realize they may need less than expected. But those people are few and far between. Unfortunately, more often, I get cases like this: A couple comes to me and says they spent X-amount a month for most of their life. After two years of retirement, though, they're horrified to realize their average monthly spending was way more than that. They're losing money faster than planned, and their "plan" is derailing. You don't want to find yourself in that situation.

Another hefty "surprise" expense is spending on the kids. Many of the couples I work with are quick to help their adult children, whether it's something like letting them live in the basement, paying for college, babysitting, paying an occasional bill, or even just contributing to a grandchild's college fund. They aren't alone—79 percent of Americans in 2018 said they had provided financial support for an adult child. And it's not unlikely for some parents to tap into their retirement funds to do so.[17]

My clients sometimes protest that what they do for their grown children can stop in retirement. They don't *need* to help. But I get it. Parents like to feel needed. And, while you never want to neglect saving for retirement in favor of taking on financial risks (like your child's student debt), the parents who help their adult children do so in part because it helps them feel fulfilled.

When it comes down to expenses, including (and especially) spending on your family, don't make your initial calculations based on what you *could* whittle your budget down to if you *had* to. Instead, start from where you are. Who wants to live off a bare-bones bank account in retirement?

---

[17] Lorie Konish. CNBC. October 2, 2018. "Parents Spend Twice as Much on Adult Children than They Save for Retirement."
https://www.cnbc.com/2018/10/02/parents-spend-twice-as-much-on-adult-children-than-saving-for-retirement.html

Other Expenses

Once you have nailed down your current budget and your dreams or goals for retirement, there are a few other outstanding pieces to think about—some expenses many people don't take the time to consider before making and executing a plan. But I'm assuming you want to get it right, so let's take a look.

Housing

Do you know where you want to live in retirement? This makes up a substantial piece of your income puzzle—since the typical American household owns a home, and it's generally their largest asset—but it often goes unaccounted for until the last minute.[18]

Some people prefer to live right where they are for as long as they can. Others have been waiting for retirement to pull the trigger on an ambitious move. Whatever your plans and whatever your reasons, there are quite a few things to consider.

Mortgage

Do you still have a mortgage? What may have been a nice tax boon in your working years could turn into a financial burden in your retirement. After all, when you are on a limited income, a mortgage is just one more bill sapping your financial strength. It is something to put some thought into, whether you plan to age in place or are considering moving to your dream home, buying a house out of state, or living in a retirement community.

---

[18] Jann Swanson. Mortgage News Daily. August 28, 2019. "Homeownership is the Top Contributor to Household Wealth." http://www.mortgagenewsdaily.com/08282019_homeownership.asp

Upkeep and Taxes

A house sans mortgage still requires annual taxes. While it's tempting to think of this as a once-a-year expense, when you have limited earning potential, your annual tax bill might be something into which you want to put a little more forethought.

The costs of homeownership aren't just monetary. When you find yourself dealing with more house than you need, it can drain your time and energy. From keeping clutter at bay to keeping the lawn mower running, upkeep can be extensive and expensive. For some, that's a challenge they heartily accept and can comfortably take on. For others, the idea of yard work or cleaning an area larger than they need feels foolish.

For instance, Peggy discovered after her knee replacement that most of her house was inaccessible to her when she was laid up.

"It felt ridiculous to pay someone else to dust and vacuum a house I was only living in 40 percent of!"

Practicality and Adaptability

Erik and Magda are looking to retire within the next two decades. They just sold their old three-bedroom ranch-style house. Their twins are in high school, and the couple has wanted to "upgrade" for years. Now they live in a gorgeous 1940s three-story house with all the kitchen space they ever wanted, five sprawling bedrooms, and a library and media room for themselves and their children. Within months of moving in, the couple realized a house perfect for their active teens would no longer be perfect for them in five to fifteen years.

"We are already paying the mortgage for this house, but we've started saving for the next one," said Magda, "Because who wants to climb up two flights of stairs to their bedroom when they're seventy-eight?"

Others I know have encountered a similar situation in their personal lives. After a health crisis, one couple found the luxurious tub for two they slaved over installing had become a specter of a bad slip and safety risks. It's important to think through what your physical reality could be, whatever your long-term plan might be, and it's amazing how many people don't.

Contracts and Regulations

If you are looking into a cross-country move, be aware of new tax tables or local ordinances in the area where you are looking to move. After all, you don't want to experience sticker-shock when you are looking at downsizing or reducing your bills in retirement.

Along the same lines, if you are moving into a retirement community, be sure to look at the fine print. What happens if you must move into a different situation for long-term care? Will you be penalized? Will you be responsible for replacing your slot in the community? What are all of the fees, and what do they cover?

Inflation

As I write this in 2020, America has experienced a long stretch of low inflation, with inflation not exceeding 4 percent since 1991.[19]

However, inflation isn't a one-time bump; it has a cumulative effect. Even with relatively low inflation over the past few decades, the $20 sneakers you bought your grade-schooler in 1991 will cost $34.02 to buy for your grandchild.[20] What if, in retirement, we hit a stretch like in the late '70s and early '80s when annual inflation rates of 10 percent became the norm? It may be wise to consider some extra padding in your

---

[19] US Inflation Calculator. January 2020. "Historical Inflation Rates." http://www.usinflationcalculator.com/inflation/historical-inflation-rates/
[20] Ibid.

retirement income plan to account for any potential increase in inflation in the future.

Aging

Also, in the expense category, think about longevity. We all hope to age gracefully. However, it's important to face the prospect of aging with a sense of realism.

The elephant in the room for many families is long-term care: No one wants to admit they will likely need it, but the reality is as many as 70 percent of us will. [21] Aging is a significant piece of retirement income planning because you'll want to figure out how to set aside money for your care, either at home or away from it. The more comfortable you get with discussing your wishes and plans with your loved ones, the easier planning for the financial side of it can be.

I discuss health care and potential long-term care costs in more detail elsewhere in this book, but, suffice it to say, nursing home care is incredibly expensive and typically not something you get to choose when you need.

It isn't just the costs of long-term care that pose a concern in living longer. It's also about covering the possible costs of everything else associated with living longer. For instance, if Henry retires from his job as a biochemical engineer at age sixty-five, perhaps he planned to have a very decent income for twenty years, until age eighty-five. But what if he lives until he's ninety-five? That's a whole third—ten years—more of personal income he will need.

---

[21] Moll Law Group. 2019. "The Cost of Long-Term Care." https://www.molllawgroup.com/the-cost-of-long-term-care.html.

Putting It All Together

Whew! So, you have pulled together what you have, and you have a pretty good idea of where you want to be. Now your financial professional and you can go about the work of arranging what assets you *have* to cover what you need—and how you might try to cover any gaps.

Like the proverbial man in the Bible who built his house on a rock, I like to help my clients figure out how to cover their day-to-day living expenses—their needs—with insurance and other guaranteed income sources, like pensions and Social Security.

To retire, you should look at your investments and savings like a pyramid. The rock-like foundation to a sound retirement is essential income. You want that money to be guaranteed, and you can't only have enough under ideal circumstances. What happens if there's a shortfall? How much of your savings or other assets would you need to sacrifice to compensate? It's best to plan for unexpected scenarios rather than for the minimum needed in ideal situations.

The next level, after the foundation is properly funded, covers discretionary spending—the extra money you should have for "want" purchases. This level includes items like a new television or a lakehouse, where unneeded funds from the first level can be put toward additional desired expenses that aren't necessary. Then there's growth money. Those funds are set aside to build over time so future long-term care costs, inheritance, and inflation are accounted for. If your investments are doing what you need them to do—that is, they satisfy each tier of the pyramid sustainably—you can retire.

Many have been indoctrinated with the over-simplified belief that to retire you only need a million dollars (or some other specific number) in savings. But it's not about savings. It's about having what you need from all available assets to sustain income.

Again, you should keep in mind there isn't one single financial vehicle, asset, or source to fill all of your needs, and that's okay. One of the challenges of making a plan for your income in retirement concerns figuring out what products to use. You can release some of that stress when you accept the fact you will need a diverse portfolio—potentially with bonds, stocks, insurance, and other income sources—not just one massive money pile.

One way to help shore up your income gaps is by working with your financial professional and a qualified tax advisor to mitigate your tax exposure. If you have a 401(k) or IRA, a financial advisor in your corner can help you figure out how and when to take distributions from your account in a way that doesn't push you into a higher tax bracket. Or you might learn how to use tax-advantaged bonds more effectively. Effective tax planning isn't necessarily about "adding" to your income; especially with retirement, it's less about what you make as it is about what you keep. Paying a lower tax bill keeps more money in your pocket, which is where you want it when it comes to retirement income.

Now you can look at ways to cover your remaining retirement goals. Are there products like long-term care insurance specific to a certain kind of expense you anticipate? Is there a particular asset you want to use for your "play" money—money for trips and gifts for the grandkids? Is there any way you can portion off money for those charitable legacy plans?

Once you have analyzed your income wants, needs, and your realistic assets to cover them, you may have a gap. The masterstroke of a competent financial professional will be to help you figure out how you will cover that gap. Will you need to cut out a round of golf a week? Maybe skip the new car? Or will you need to take more substantial action?

One way to cover an income gap is to consider working longer or even part-time before retirement and even after that magical calendar date. This may not be the best "plan" for you;

disabilities, work demands, and physical or emotional limitations can hinder the best-laid plans to continue working. However, if it is physically possible for you, this is one considerable way to help your assets last, for more than one reason.

In fact, about one in five Americans are still working past age sixty-five. This is a record percentage in the past half-century. While some do list their personal finances as a reason for staying on the job, others do so to avoid feeling bored in retirement, among other reasons.[22]

When you're retired, you no longer have an employer paying you a steady check. It is up to you to make sure you have saved and planned for the income you need.

---

[22] Associated Press. October 9, 2018. "1 in 5 Americans over 65 are Still Waiting to Retire." https://nypost.com/2018/10/09/1-in-5-americans-over-65-are-still-waiting-to-retire/

CHAPTER 5

Social Security

Social Security is often the foundation piece of retirement income. Backed by the strength of the U.S. Treasury, it provides perhaps the most dependable paycheck you will have in retirement.

From the time you collect your first paycheck at whatever job made you a bonafide taxpayer (for me, it was throwing newspapers with my mom in Concord, California), you are paying into the grand old Social Security system. What grew and developed out of the pressures of the Great Depression has become one of the most popular government programs in the country, and, if you pay in the equivalent of ten years or more, you, too, can benefit from the Social Security program.

Now, before we get into the nitty-gritty of Social Security, I'd like to address a current concern: Will Social Security still be there for you when you reach retirement age?

The Future of Social Security

This question is ever-present as headlines trumpet an underfunded Social Security program alongside the flux of baby boomers who are retiring in droves, and the comparatively smaller younger generations who are bearing the responsibility of funding the system.

The Social Security Administration itself is a source of this concern as each Social Security statement now bears an asterisk that continues near the end of the summary:

*"*Your estimated benefits are based on current law. Congress has made changes to the law in the past and can do so at any time. The law governing benefit amounts may change because, by 2034, the payroll taxes collected will be enough to pay only about 79 percent of scheduled benefits."*

Just a reminder, as if you needed one, that nothing in life is guaranteed.

Before you get too discouraged, though, here are a few thoughts to keep you going:

- Although those who retire after 2034 may only receive 79 cents on the dollar for their scheduled benefits, 79 percent is notably not zero.
- Social Security has made changes in the distant and near past to protect the fund's solvency, including increasing retirement ages and striking certain filing strategies.
- There are many changes Congress could make, and lawmakers are currently discussing how to fix the system, such as further increasing full retirement age and eligibility.
- One thing no one is seriously discussing? Reneging on current obligations to retirees or the soon-to-retire.

Take heart. The real answer to the question, "Will Social Security be there for me?" is still "yes."

This question is an important one to consider when you take a look at how much we, as a nation, rely on this program. Did you know Social Security benefits replace about 40 percent of a person's original income when they retire?[23]

If you ask me, that's a pretty significant piece of your retirement income puzzle.

Another caveat? You may not realize this, but no one can legally "advise" you about your Social Security benefits.

"But, Chad," you may be thinking, "Isn't that part of what you do? And what about that nice gentleman at the Social Security Administration office I spoke with on the phone?"

Don't get me wrong. Social Security Administration employees know their stuff. They are trained to know policies and programs, and they are usually pretty quick to tell you what you can and cannot do. But the government specifically says, because Social Security is a benefit you alone have paid into and earned, your Social Security decisions, too, are yours alone.

When it comes to financial professionals, we can't push you in any directions, either, *but*—there's a big but here—working with a well-informed financial professional is still incredibly handy when it comes to your Social Security decisions. Why? Because someone who's worth his or her salt will know what withdrawal strategies might pertain to your specific situation and will ask questions that can help you determine what you are looking for when it comes to your Social Security.

For instance, some people want the highest possible monthly benefit. Others want to start their benefits early, not always because of financial need. I heard about one man who called in to start his Social Security payments the day he qualified, just because he liked to think of it as the government paying back a debt it owed him, and he enjoyed the feeling of receiving a check from Uncle Sam.

Whatever your reasons, questions, or feelings regarding Social Security, the decision is yours alone; but working with a financial professional can help you put your options in perspective by showing you—both with industry knowledge and

---

[23] Social Security Administration. "Learn About Social Security Programs." https://www.ssa.gov/planners/retire/r&m6.html

with proprietary software or planning processes—where your benefits fit into your overall strategy for retirement income.

One reason the federal government doesn't allow for "advice" related to Social Security, I suspect, is so no one can profit from giving you advice related to your Social Security benefit—or from providing any clarifications. Again, this is a sign of a good financial professional. Those who are passionate about their work will be knowledgeable about what benefit strategies might be to your advantage and will happily share those possible options with you.

Full Retirement Age

When it comes to Social Security, it seems like many people only think so far as "yes." They don't take the time to understand the various options available. Instead, because it is common knowledge you can begin your benefits at age sixty-two, that's what many of us do. While more people are opting to delay taking benefits, age sixty-two is still firmly the most popular age to start.[24]

What many people fail to understand is, by starting benefits early, they may be leaving a lot of money on the table. You see, the Social Security Administration bases your monthly benefit on two factors: your earnings history and your full retirement age (FRA).

From your earnings history, they pull the thirty-five years you made the most money and use a mathematical indexing formula to figure out a monthly average from those years. If you paid into the system for less than thirty-five years, then every year you didn't pay in will be counted as a zero.

---

24 Elizabeth O'Brien. Money. March 7, 2019. "This is the Age when Most People Claim Social Security—and When Experts Say You Really Should." http://money.com/money/5637694/this-is-the-age-when-most-people-claim-social-security-and-when-experts-say-you-really-should/

Once they have calculated what your monthly earning would be at FRA, the government then calculates what to put on your check based on how close you are to FRA. FRA was originally set at sixty-five, but, as the population aged and lifespans lengthened, the government shifted FRA later and later based on an individual's year of birth. Check out the following chart to see when you will reach FRA.[25]

---

[25] Social Security Administration. "Full Retirement Age." https://www.ssa.gov/planners/retire/retirechart.html

Age to Receive Full Social Security Benefits*	
(Called "full retirement age" [FRA] or "normal retirement age.")	
Year of Birth*	FRA
1937 or earlier	65
1938	65 and 2 months
1939	65 and 4 months
1940	65 and 6 months
1941	65 and 8 months
1942	65 and 10 months
1943-1954	66
1955	66 and 2 months
1956	66 and 4 months
1957	66 and 6 months
1958	66 and 8 months
1959	66 and 10 months
1960 and later	67
**If you were born on Jan. 1 of any year, you should refer to the previous year. (If you were born on the 1st of the month, we figure your benefit [and your full retirement age] as if your birthday was in the previous month.)*	

When you attain FRA, you are eligible to receive 100 percent of whatever the Social Security Administration says is your full monthly benefit.

Starting at age sixty-two, for every year before FRA you claim benefits, your monthly check is reduced by 5 percent. Conversely, for every year you delay taking benefits past FRA, your monthly benefit increases by 8 percent (until age seventy—after that, there is no monetary advantage to delaying Social Security benefits). While your circumstances and needs may vary, this is why a lot of financial professionals urge people to at least consider delaying until they reach age seventy.

Why Wait? [26]

Taking benefits early could affect your monthly check by ______.								
62	63	64	65	FRA 66	67	68	69	70
-20 %	-15 %	-10 %	-5 %	0	+8 %	+16 %	+24 %	+32 %

My Social Security

As long as you are over age thirty, you have probably received a notice from the Social Security Administration telling you to activate something called "My Social Security." This is a handy way to learn more about your particular benefit options, to keep track of what your earnings record looks like, and to calculate the benefits you have accrued over the years.

Essentially, My Social Security is an online account you can activate to see what your personal Social Security picture looks like, which you can do at www.ssa.gov/myaccount. This can be extremely helpful when it comes to planning for income in retirement and figuring up the difference between your anticipated income versus anticipated expenses.

My Social Security is also helpful because it's a great way to see if there is a problem. For instance, I have heard of one woman who, through diligently checking her tax records against her Social Security profile, discovered her Social

---

[26] Social Security Administration. April 2019. "Can You Take Your Benefits Before Full Retirement Age?"
https://www.ssa.gov/planners/retire/applying2.html

Security check was shortchanging her, based on her earnings history. After taking the discrepancy to the Social Security Administration, they sent her what they owed her in makeup benefits.

COLA

Social Security is a largely guaranteed piece of the retirement puzzle: If you get a statement that says to expect $1,000 a month, you can be sure you will receive $1,000 a month. But there is one variable detail, and that is something called the cost-of-living adjustment, or COLA.

The COLA is an increase in your monthly check meant to address inflation in everyday life. After all, your expenses will likely continue to experience inflation in retirement, but you will no longer have the opportunity for raises, bonuses, or promotions you had when you were working. Instead, Social Security receives an annual cost-of-living increase tied to the Department of Labor's Consumer Price Index for Urban Wage Earners and Clerical Workers, or CPI-W. If the CPI-W measurement shows inflation rose a certain amount for regular goods and services, then Social Security recipients will see that reflected in their COLA.

The COLA averages 4 percent, but in a no- or low-inflation environment, such as in 2010, 2011, and 2016, Social Security recipients will not receive an adjustment. Some view the COLA as a perk, bump, or bonus, but, in reality, it works more like this: Your mom sends you to the store with $2.50 for a gallon of milk. Milk costs exactly $2.50. The next week, you go back with that same amount, but it is now $2.52 for a gallon, so you go back to Mom, and she gives you 2 cents. You aren't bringing home more milk—it just costs more money.

So the COLA is less about "making" more money and more about keeping seniors' purchasing power from eroding when inflation is a big factor, such as in 1975, when it was 8 percent!

[27] Still, don't let that detract from your enthusiasm about COLAs; after all, what if Mom's solution was: "Here's the same $2.50; try to find pennies from somewhere else to get that milk!"?

Spousal Benefits

We've talked about FRA, but another big Social Security decision involves spousal benefits.

If you or your spouse has a long stretch of zeros in your earnings history—perhaps if one of you stayed home for years, caring for children or sick relatives—you may want to consider filing for spousal benefits instead of filing on your own earnings history. A spousal benefit can be up to 50 percent of the primary wage earner's benefit at full retirement age.

To begin drawing a spousal benefit, you must be at least sixty-two years old, and the primary wage earner must have already filed for his or her benefit. While there are penalties for taking spousal benefits early (you could lose up to 67.5 percent of your check for filing at age sixty-two), you cannot earn credits for delaying past full retirement age.[28]

Like I said, the spousal benefit can be a big deal for those who don't have a very long pay history, but it's important to weigh your own earned benefits against the option of withdrawing based on a fraction of your spouse's benefits.

To look at how this could play out, let's use a hypothetical example of Mary Jane, who is sixty, and Peter, who is sixty-two.

Let's say Peter's benefit at FRA, in his case sixty-six, would be $1,600. If Peter begins his benefits right now, four years before FRA, his monthly check will be $1,200. If Mary Jane begins taking spousal benefits in two years, at the earliest date

---

[27] Social Security Administration. "Cost-Of-Living Adjustment (COLA) Information for 2019." https://www.ssa.gov/cola/

[28] Social Security Administration. "Retirement Planner: Benefits For You As A Spouse." https://www.ssa.gov/planners/retire/applying6.html

possible, her monthly benefits will be reduced by 67.5 percent, to $520 per month (remember, at FRA, the most she can qualify for is half of Peter's FRA benefit).

What if Peter and Mary Jane both wait until FRA? At sixty-six, Peter begins taking his full benefit of $1,600 a month. Two years later, when she reaches age sixty-six, Mary Jane will qualify for $800 a month. By waiting until FRA, the couple's monthly benefit goes from $1,720 to $2,400.

What if Peter delays until age seventy to take his maximum possible benefit? For each year past FRA he delays, his monthly benefits increase by 8 percent. This means, at seventy, he could file for a monthly benefit of $2,112. However, delayed retirement credits do not affect spousal benefits, so, as soon as Peter files at seventy, Mary Jane would also file (at age sixty-eight) for her maximum benefit of $800, making their highest possible combined monthly check $2,912.[29]

When it comes to your Social Security benefits, you obviously will want to consider if a monthly check based on a fraction of your spouse's earnings will be comparable to or larger than your own earnings history.

I've thrown a lot of numbers at you to consider, like your FRA based on your year of birth, as well as COLA and spousal benefits (and we haven't even gotten to taxes!), but here's another date to think about: Jan. 2, 1954. What's important about that, you ask? For those born on or after that date, you can only make the choice to withdraw your benefits one way, one time. That means you will have to pick whether to take a spousal benefit or use your own earnings history, and whichever one you choose will be the check you get every month for the duration of your retirement. However, if you were born *before* Jan. 2, 1954, read on.

If you were born before Jan. 2, 1954, you are eligible to change your benefit withdrawal strategy *even after you have*

---

[29] Office of the Chief Actuary. Social Security Administration. 2017. "Social Security Benefits: Benefits for Spouses."
https://www.ssa.gov/OACT/quickcalc/spouse.html#calculator

begun withdrawals. This means you could begin taking a spousal benefit at sixty-two or at FRA while allowing the benefits based on your own earnings history to accrue.[30]

Let's look back to Mary Jane and Peter to see how this could theoretically work. We know, if they both file at FRA, Mary Jane will receive $800 a month on top of Peter's $1,600 benefit when she files. But, what if her own earned credit at FRA was $700? In four years, when Mary Jane turns seventy, the monthly benefit based on her personal earnings will have grown from $700 to $924. At seventy, she could file to trade up her $800 monthly spousal benefit for a $924 monthly check. Remember, this only works for Mary Jane if she was born before Jan. 2, 1954.

Divorced Spouses

There are a few considerations for those of us who have gone through a divorce. If you 1) were married for ten years or more *and* 2) have since been divorced for at least two years *and* 3) are unmarried *and* 4) your ex-spouse qualifies to begin Social Security, you qualify for a spousal benefit based on your ex-husband or ex-wife's earnings history at FRA. A divorced spousal benefit is different from the married spousal benefit in one way: You don't have to wait for your ex-spouse to file before you can file yourself.[31]

For instance, Charles and Moira were married for fifteen years before their divorce, when he was thirty-six and she was forty. Moira has been remarried for twenty years, and, although Charles briefly remarried, his second marriage ended after a few years. Charles' benefits are largely calculated based on his

---

[30] Social Security Administration. "Retirement Planner: Benefits For You As A Spouse." https://www.ssa.gov/planners/retire/applying6.html
[31] Social Security Administration. "Retirement Planner: If You Are Divorced." https://www.ssa.gov/planners/retire/divspouse.html

many years of volunteering in schools, meaning his personal monthly benefit is close to zero.

Although Moira has deferred her retirement, opting to delay benefits until she is seventy, Charles can begin taking benefits calculated off of Moira's work history at FRA as early as sixty-two. However, he will also have the option of waiting until FRA to collect the maximum, 50 percent, of Moira's earned monthly benefit at her FRA.

Widowed Spouses

If your marriage ended with the death of your spouse, you might claim a benefit for your spouse's earned income as his or her widow/widower, called a survivor's benefit. Unlike a spousal benefit or divorced benefits, if your husband or wife dies, you are allowed to claim his or her full benefit. Also unlike spousal benefits, if you need to, you can begin taking income when you turn sixty. However, as with other benefit options, your monthly check will be permanently reduced for withdrawing benefits before FRA.

If your spouse began taking benefits before he or she died, you can't delay withdrawing your survivor's benefits to get delayed credits; the Social Security Administration says you can only get as much from a survivor's benefit as what your deceased spouse might have gotten, had he or she lived.[32]

Taxes, Taxes, Taxes

With Social Security, as with everything, it is important to consider taxes. It may be surprising, but your Social Security benefits are not tax-free. Despite having been taxed to accrue

---

[32] Social Security Administration. "Social Security Benefit Amounts For The Surviving Spouse By Year Of Birth."
https://www.ssa.gov/planners/survivors/survivorchartred.html

those benefits in the first place, you may have to pay Uncle Sam income taxes on up to 85 percent of your Social Security.

The way the Social Security Administration figures these taxes is what they call "the provisional income formula." Your provisional income formula differs from the adjusted gross income you use for your regular income taxes. Instead, to find out how much of your Social Security benefit is taxable, the Social Security Administration calculates it this way:

Provisional Income = Adjusted Gross Income + Nontaxable Interest + ½ of Social Security

See that piece about nontaxable interest? That generally means interest from government bonds and notes. It surprises many people that, although you may not pay taxes on those assets, their income will count against you when it comes to Social Security taxation.

Once you have figured out your provisional income (also called "combined income"), you can use the following chart to figure out your Social Security taxes.[33]

---

[33] Social Security Administration. "Benefits Planner: Income Taxes and Your Social Security Benefits." https://www.ssa.gov/planners/taxes.html

Taxes on Social Security		
Provisional Income = Adjusted Gross Income + Nontaxable Interest + ½ of Social Security		
If you are ____ and your provisional income is____, then...		Uncle Sam will tax ___ of your Social Security
Single	Married, filing jointly	
Less than $25,000	Less than $32,000	0%
$25,000 to $34,000	$32,000 to $44,000	Up to 50%
More than $34,000	More than $44,000	Up to 85%

This is one more reason it may benefit you to work with a financial professional: He or she can take a look at your entire picture to make your overall retirement plan as tax-efficient as possible—including your Social Security benefit.

Often, people come to our Social Security seminars wanting to find out at what age they should take Social Security. It's impossible to give an ideal number for every retiree, and the decision is truly up to the individual. Your personal circumstances ultimately dictate what's best for you, but, in many cases, it's more tax-efficient to delay collecting Social Security, wait until you reach a higher Social Security benefit, and live off your IRA in the meantime. However, all individuals are encouraged to seek the guidance of a qualified tax professional regarding their personal situation.

Working and Social Security: The Earnings Test

If you haven't reached FRA, but you started your Social Security benefits and are still working, things get a little hairy.

Because you have started Social Security payments, the Social Security Administration will pay out your benefits (docked, of course, for what you could have gotten if you had waited to file until your FRA). Yet, because you are working, the organization must also withhold from your check to add to your benefits . . . which you are already collecting. See how this complicates matters?

To straighten the situation, the government has what is called "the earnings test." For 2020, you can earn up to $18,240 without it affecting your Social Security check. But for every $2 you earn past that amount, the Social Security Administration will withhold $1. The earnings test loosens in the year of your FRA; if you are reaching FRA in 2020, you can earn up to $48,600 before you run into the earnings test, and the government only withholds $1 for every $3 past that amount. In the month you reach FRA, you are no longer subject to any earnings withholding. For instance, if you are still working and will turn sixty-six on December 28, 2020, you would only have to worry about the earnings test until December, and then you can ignore it entirely. Keep in mind, the money the government withholds from your Social Security benefits while you are working before FRA will be tacked back onto your benefits check after FRA.[34]

Social Security is a huge piece of the retirement planning process. For many (if not most) retirees, Social Security is their only source of guaranteed income. So, as you make every other decision, be sure to consider how it could affect your Social

---

[34] Social Security Administration. "Exempt Amounts Under the Earnings Test." https://www.ssa.gov/oact/cola/rtea.html

Security. If you can wait long enough for your Social Security to grow, it might be worth it.

Sometimes, people come to my seminar and say they have a financial advisor already, but they came just to figure out how Social Security works. I'm sorry, what? How can anyone claim to be a financial advisor who gives investment advice if they don't understand how Social Security works? It factors into every other decision a retiree should make. Please, make sure your financial advisor understands the gravity of Social Security planning before handing over to him or her the authority to care for your assets.

CHAPTER 6

401(k)s & IRAs

Have you heard? Today's retirement is not your dad's retirement. You see, back in the day, it was pretty common to work for one company for the vast majority of your career and then retire with a gold watch and a pension.

The gold watch was a symbol of the quality time you had put in at that company, but the pension was more than a symbol. Instead, it was a guarantee—as solid as your employer—that they would repay your hard work with a certain amount of income in your old age. Did you see the caveat there? Your pension's guarantee was *as solid as your employer*. The problem was, what if your employer went under?

Companies that failed couldn't pay their retired employees' pensions, leading to financial challenges for many. Beginning in 1974 with Congress' passage of the Employee Retirement Income Security Act, federal legislation and regulations aimed at protecting retirees were everywhere. One piece of legislation included a relatively obscure section of the Internal Revenue Code, added in 1978. Section 401(k), to be specific.

IRC section 401, subsection k, created tax advantages for employer-sponsored financial products, even if the main contributor was the employee him or herself. Over the years, more employers took note, beginning an age of transition away from pensions and toward 401(k) plans. A 401(k) is a retirement account with certain tax benefits and restrictions on the investments or other financial products inside of it.

Essentially, 401(k)s and their individual retirement account (IRA) counterparts are "wrappers" that provide tax benefits around assets; typically the assets that compose IRAs and 401(k)s are mutual funds, stock and bond mixes, and money market accounts. However, IRA and 401(k) contents are becoming more diverse these days, with some companies offering different kinds of annuity options within their plans.

Where pensions are defined-*benefit* plans, 401(k)s and IRAs counterparts are defined-*contribution* plans. The one-word change outlines the basic difference. Pensions spell out what you can expect to receive from the plan, but not necessarily how much money it will take to fund those benefits. With 401(k)s, an employer sets a standard for how much they will contribute (if any), and you can be certain of what you are contributing. Still, there is no outline for what you can expect to receive in return for those contributions.

Modern employment looks very different these days. A 2018 survey by the Bureau of Labor Statistics determined U.S. workers stayed with their employers a median of about four years. Workers ages fifty-five to sixty-four had a little more staying power and were most likely to stay with their employer for about ten years.[35] Additionally, in 1979, when those employees would have been hitting their strides, career-wise, 38 percent of workers had pensions. But 401(k)s are rising in number, with about 55 million American workers enrolled in a plan.[36]

A far cry from a pension and gold watch, wouldn't you say?

If you do have a pension, congratulations. Planning with one can be pretty easy. You've got a built-in monthly check. Like I've

---

[35] Bureau of Labor Statistics. September 20,2018. "Employee Tenure Summary." https://www.bls.gov/news.release/tenure.nro.htm

[36] Investment Company Institute. December 31, 2018. "Frequently Asked Questions about 401(k) Plan Research." https://www.ici.org/policy/retirement/plan/401k/faqs_401k

said many times already, retirement isn't about a pile of money. It's about developing income. But with fewer than 40 percent of Americans retiring with a pension, few accomplish this so easily.[37] Many still think they'll retire like previous generations, but we're now seeing the first group of retirees who are almost entirely responsible for their own income.

If there is anything to learn from this paradigm shift, it's that you have to look out for you. Whether you have worked for a company for two years or twenty, you are still the one who has to look out for your own best interests. That holds doubly true when it comes to preparing for retirement. If you are one of the lucky ones who still has a pension, good for you. But for the rest of us, it is likely a 401(k)—or possibly one of its nonprofit- or government-sector counterparts, a 403(b) or 457 plan—is one of your biggest assets for retirement.

Some employers offer incentives to contribute to their company plans, like a company match. On that subject, I have one thing to say: *do it!* Nothing in life is free, as they say, but a company match on your retirement funds is about as close to free money as I think it gets. If you can make the minimum to qualify for your company's match at all, go for it.

Now, it's likely, during our working years, we mostly "set and forget" our 401(k) funding. Because it is tax-advantaged, your employer is taking money from your paycheck—before taxes— and putting it into your plan for you. Maybe you got to pick a selection of investments, or maybe your company only offers one choice of investment in your 401(k). Either way, while you are gainfully employed, your most impactful decision may just be the decision to continue funding your plan in the first place. But, when you are ready to retire or move jobs, you have choices to make requiring a little more thought and care.

---

[37] Pension Rights Center. July 15, 2019. "How Many American Workers Participate in Workplace Retirement Plans?" https://www.pensionrights.org/publications/statistic/how-many-american-workers-participate-workplace-retirement-plans

When you are ready to part ways with your job, you have a few options:

- Leave the money where it is
- Take the cash (and pay income taxes and perhaps a 10 percent additional federal tax if you are younger than age fifty-nine-and-one-half)
- Transfer the money to another employer plan (if the new plan allows)
- Roll the money over into a self-directed IRA

Now, these are just general options. You will have to decide, hopefully with the help of a financial professional, what's right for you. For instance, 401(k)s are typically pretty closely tied to the companies offering them, so, when changing jobs, it may not always be possible to transfer a 401(k) to another 401(k). Leaving the money where it is may also be out of the question—some companies have direct cash payout or rollover policies once someone is no longer employed.

Remember what we said earlier about how we change jobs more often these days? That means you likely have a 401(k) with your current company, but you may also have a string of IRAs trailing you from other jobs.

A fairly new client of mine illustrates this situation well. He has *twelve* different retirement accounts—IRAs, 401(k)s, and 457s—all over the place. He has wanted to retire for some time but has felt unqualified. This guy just hadn't done the footwork to piece all his assets together.

The "problem" was this gentleman had job-hopped often and experienced company acquisitions and merges over forty years of his career. His string of retirement accounts was more jumbled than the legendary Gordian Knot. It took him and his wife about three of four visits to believe it when I explained to them just how much they had—and that they could retire immediately if they chose.

When it comes to your retirement income, it's important to be able to pull together *all* of your assets, so you can examine what you have and where.

Tax-Qualified, Tax-Preferred, Tax-Deferred . . . Still TAXED

Financial media often cite IRAs and 401(k)s for their tax benefits. After all, with traditional plans, you put your money in, pre-tax, and it hopefully grows for years, even decades, untaxed. That's why these accounts are called "tax-qualified" or "tax-deferred" assets. They aren't *tax-free*! Rarely does Uncle Sam allow business to continue without receiving his piece of the pie, and your retirement assets are no different. If you didn't pay taxes on the front end, you will pay taxes on the money you withdraw from these accounts in retirement. Don't get me wrong: This isn't an inherently bad thing, nor is it a good thing; it's just the way it is. It's important to understand, though, for the sake of planning ahead.

In retirement, many people assume they will be in a lower tax bracket. Are you planning to pare down your lifestyle in retirement? Perhaps you are, and perhaps you will have substantially less income in retirement. But many of my clients tell me they want to live life more or less the same as they always have. The money they would previously have spent on business attire or gas for their commute they now want to spend on hobbies and grandchildren. That's all fine, and, for many of them, it is doable, but does it put them in a lower tax bracket? No.

Because of their special tax status, IRAs, 401(k)s, and their alternatives have a few limitations you should understand. For one thing, the IRS sets limits on your contributions to these retirement accounts. If you are contributing to a 401(k) or an equivalent nonprofit or government plan, your annual contribution limit is $19,500 (as of 2020). If you are fifty or older, the IRS allows additional contributions, called "catch-up contributions," of up to $6,500 on top of the regular limit of $19,500. For an IRA, the limit is $6,000, with a catch-up limit of an additional $1,000.[38]

Because their tax advantages come from their intended use as retirement income, withdrawing funds from these accounts before you turn fifty-nine-and-one-half can carry stiff penalties. In addition to fees your investment management company might charge, you will have to pay income tax *and* a 10 percent federal tax penalty.

Now, there are a few exceptions to the fifty-nine-and-one-half rule such as medical expenses or disability, but generally it is incredibly important to remember, especially when you're young. [39] Younger workers are often tempted to cash out an IRA from a previous employer and then are surprised to find their checks missing 20 percent of the account value to income taxes, penalty taxes, and account fees.

It's also important to keep in mind the fifty-nine-and-one-half rule for younger workers because many millennials I see in my practice come in and, while they may be socking money away in their workplace retirement plan, it's often the *only* place they are saving. This could be problematic later because of the fifty-nine-and-one-half rule. What if you have an emergency? It is important to fund your retirement, but you need to have some liquid assets handy as emergency funds. This can help you avoid breaking into your retirement accounts and incurring taxes and penalties as a result of the fifty-nine-and-one-half rule.

---

[38] Troy Segal. Investopedia. January 17, 2020. "What Are the Roth 401(k) Contribution Limits." https://www.investopedia.com/ask/answers/102714/what-are-roth-401k-contibution-limits.asp

[39] IRS. October 29, 2019. "Retirement Topics: Exceptions to Tax on Early Distributions." https://www.irs.gov/retirement-plans/plan-participant-employee/retirement-topics-tax-on-early-distributions

RMDs

Remember how we talked about the 401(k) or IRA being a "tax wrapper" for your funds? Well, eventually, Uncle Sam will want a bite of that candy bar. So, beginning at age seventy-two, the government requires you withdraw a portion of your account, which they calculate based on the size of your account and your estimated lifespan. This required minimum distribution—or RMD—is the government's insurance it will collect some taxes, at some point, from your earnings. Because you didn't pay taxes on the front end, you will now pay income taxes on whatever you withdraw, including your RMDs. *Also*, let me just remind you not to play chicken with the U.S. government; if you don't take your RMDs starting at age seventy-two, you will have to write a check to the IRS for 50 *percent* of the amount of your missed RMDs.

If you don't need income from your retirement accounts, RMDs can seem like more of a tax burden than an income boon. While some people prefer to reinvest their RMDs, this comes with the possibility of additional taxation: You'll pay income taxes on your RMDs and then capital gains taxes on the growth of your investments. If you are legacy minded, there are other ways to use RMDs, many of which have tax benefits.

Permanent Life Insurance

One way to turn those pesky RMDs into a legacy is through permanent life insurance. If properly structured, these products avoid taxation and can pass on a sizeable death benefit to your beneficiaries, tax-free, as part of your general legacy plan.

ILIT

Another way to use RMDs toward your legacy is to work with an estate planning attorney to create an irrevocable life insurance trust (ILIT). This is basically a permanent life insurance policy held within a trust. Because the trust is irrevocable, you would relinquish control of it, but, unlike a stand-alone permanent life insurance policy, your death benefit won't count toward your taxable estate.

Annuities

Because annuities can be tax-deferred, using your RMDs to fund an annuity contract can be one way to further delay taxation while guaranteeing your income payments (either to you or your loved ones) later.

Qualified Charitable Distributions

If you are charity-minded, you may use your RMDs toward a charitable organization instead of using them for income. You must do this directly from your retirement account (you can't take the RMD check and *then* pay the charity) for your withdrawals to be qualified charitable distributions (QCDs), but this is one way of realizing some of the benefits of a charitable legacy during your own lifetime. You will not need to pay taxes on your QCDs, and they won't count toward your annual charitable tax deduction limit, plus you'll be able to see how the organization you are supporting uses your donations. It is advisable to consult a financial professional on how to correctly make a QCD, particularly since the SECURE Act of 2019 has implemented a few minor regulations on this point.[40]

Roth

Since the Taxpayer Relief Act of 1997, there has been a different kind of retirement account, or "tax wrapper," available to the

---

[40] Bob Carlson. Forbes. January 28,2020. "More Questions And Answers About The SECURE Act."
https://www.forbes.com/sites/bobcarlson/2020/01/28/more-questions-and-answers-about-the-secure-act/#113d49564869

public: the Roth. Roth IRAs and Roth 401(k)s each differ from their traditional counterparts in one big way: You pay your taxes on the front end. This means, once your post-tax money is in the Roth account, as long as you follow the rules and limitations of that account, your distributions are truly tax-free. You won't pay income tax when you take withdrawals if the account has been open for at least 5 years, so, in turn, you don't have to worry about RMDs. However, Roth accounts have the same limitations as traditional 401(k)s and IRAs when it comes to withdrawing money before age fifty-nine-and-one-half—you'll pay a 10 percent federal penalty.

Commonly, people store all their money in traditional IRAs and 401(k)s (because that's what they've been told to do) with the assumption they'll be in a lower tax bracket after retirement. But, for a lot of folks, that's probably not true. Many could find themselves in a higher tax bracket or at least the same one they have been in for their later working life. It takes time to explain to people that they can pull money out of those accounts over time and contribute to a Roth IRA, which has a *known* tax rate, that could be lower than it would be in the future.

A common misconception about Roth IRAs is that there's a contribution limit. However, that is only true for new Roth IRAs, not Roth conversions! One client said her former finance guy advised against a Roth conversion because the time-compounded value of the tax-deferred money would never be recovered. The gain is bigger in the traditional IRA, right? Wrong! All else being equal, the value accrued would be exactly the same—but that really only reflects the best-case scenario.

Still, people get hung up on the account balance. In a traditional IRA, people neglect to realize not all that money belongs to you! Much of it belongs to the government, you just haven't had to fork it over yet.

Tax diversification is another benefit to the Roth. Even if you don't convert all your money, it can give you an additional nest egg of after-tax money you can pull from without paying taxes—whatever the current rate might be.

Taking Charge

As mentioned earlier, the 401(k) and IRA have largely replaced pensions, but they aren't an equal trade.

Pensions are employer-funded; the money feeding them is money that wouldn't ever show up on your pay stub. Because 401(k)s are self-funded, you have to actively and consciously save. This distinction has made a difference when it comes to funding retirement. According to one NerdWallet article, the average 401(k) balance for a person age sixty to sixty-nine is $198,600, but the median likely tells the full story. The median 401(k) balance for a person age sixty to sixty-nine is $63,000. The article also cites the general suggestion to aim, by age thirty, to have saved up an amount equal to 50 percent to 100 percent of your annual salary.[41] For some thirty-year-olds, saving half an annual salary by age thirty is more than some sixty-to-sixty-nine-year-olds have saved for their entire lives.

There can be many reasons people underfund their retirement plans, like being overwhelmed by the investment choices or taking withdrawals from IRAs when they leave an employer, but I believe the reason at the top of the list is this: People simply aren't participating to begin with.

So, whether you have a 401(k) with an employer or have an IRA alternative with a private company, separate from your workplace, the most important retirement savings decision you can make is to sock away your money somewhere in the first place.

---

[41] Arielle O'Shea. Nerd Wallet. January 24, 2019. "The Average 401(k) Balance by Age." https://www.nerdwallet.com/article/investing/the-average-401k-balance-by-age

CHAPTER 7

Annuities

In my practice, I offer my clients a variety of products—from securities to insurance—all designed to help them reach their financial goals. You may be wondering: Why single out a single product in this book?

Well, while most of my clients have a pretty good understanding of business and finance, I sometimes find those who have the impression there must be magic involved. Like turning straw into gold, a harp and a goose that lays golden eggs, or like Jack and the Beanstalk going from a cow to a bean to a sack of gold, some people assume there is a magic finance wand we can wave to change years' worth of savings into a strategy for retirement income.

Yet, finances aren't magic; it takes lots of hard work and, typically, several financial products and strategies to pull together a complete retirement plan. Of all the financial products I work with, it seems people find none more mysterious than annuities. And, if I may say, even some of those who recognize the word "annuity" have a limited understanding of the product. So, in the interest of demystifying annuities, let me tell you a little about what an annuity is.

Generally speaking, insurance is a financial hedge against risk. Car owners buy auto insurance to protect their finances in case they injure someone or someone injures them. Homeowners have house insurance to protect their finances in case of a fire, flood, or another disaster. People also have life insurance to protect their finances in case of untimely death. Almost juxtaposed to life insurance, people have annuities in case of a long life; by providing consistent and reliable income payments, annuities can help with financial protection.

The basic premise of an annuity is you, the annuitant, pay an insurance company some amount in exchange for their contractual guarantee they will pay you income for a certain period of time. How that company pays you, for how long, and how much they offer are determined by the annuity contract you enter into with the insurance company.

How You Get Paid

There are two ways for an annuity contract to provide income: The first is through what is called annuitization, and the second is through the use of income riders. We'll get into income riders in a bit, but let's talk about annuitization. That nice, long word is, in my opinion, one reason annuities have a reputation for mystery and misinformation.

Annuitization

When someone "annuitizes" a contract, it is the point where he or she turns on the income stream. Once a contract has been annuitized, there is no going back. With annuitites, if the policyholder lives longer than the insurance company planned, the insurance company is still obligated to pay him or her, even if the payments end up being way more than the contract's actual value. If, however, the policyholder dies an untimely death, depending on the contract type, the insurance company may keep anything left of the money that funded the annuity— nothing would be paid out to the contract holder's survivors. You see where that could make some people balk?

At a high level, here's how it looks from the insurance company's side: Numerous people will buy annuities throughout the years and begin collecting income. Some will live longer and collect more payments than others. Some may break even and receive back all that they put in, and some may pass away before receiving their full value. The company prices the annuities with this information in mind. In addition, insurance companies invest the premiums they receive from annuity holders

Now, I show you this to help explain the original concept of annuitization and how it works, from the perspectives of both an insurer and a contract holder. Modern annuities have so many bells and whistles the picture I just described seems too simplified to do them justice, but it's important to at least have a basic concept of annuitization.

Riders

Speaking of bells and whistles, let's talk about riders. Modern annuities have a lot of different options these days, many in the form of riders you can add to your contract for a fee—usually about 1 percent of the contract value per year. Each rider has its particularities, and the types of riders available will vary by the type of annuity contract purchased, but I'll just briefly outline some of these little extras:

- Lifetime income rider: Contract guarantees you an enhanced income for life
- Death benefit rider: Contract pays an enhanced death benefit to your beneficiaries even if you have annuitized
- Return of premium rider: Guarantees you (or your beneficiaries) will at least receive back the premium value of the annuity
- Long-term care rider: Provides a certain amount, sometimes as much as twice the principal value of the

contract, to help pay for long-term care if the contract holder is moved to a nursing home or assisted living situation. These riders usually pay benefits for a specified amount of time, such as 3-5 years.

This isn't an extensive look, and usually the riders have fancier names based on the issuing company, like "Lorem Ipsum Insurance Company Income Preferred Bonus Fixed Index Annuity rider," but I just wanted to show you what some of the general options are in layman's terms.

Types of Annuities

Annuities break down into four basic types: immediate, variable, fixed, and fixed index.

Immediate

Immediate annuities are not terribly popular because they primarily rely on annuitization to provide income—you give the insurance company a lump sum upfront, and your payments begin immediately. Once you begin receiving income payments, the transaction is irreversible and you no longer have access to your money in a lump sum. When you die, any remaining contract value is typically forfeited to the insurance company.

All other annuity contract types are "deferred" contracts, meaning you fund your policy as a lump sum or over a period of years and you give it the opportunity to grow over time—sometimes years, sometimes decades.

Variable

A variable annuity is an insurance contract as well as an investment. It's sold by insurance companies, but only through someone who is registered to sell investment products. With a variable annuity contract, the insurance company pools the money it receives from annuity holders and invests in investment options called sub-accounts, which in turn invest in the market. This makes it a bit different from the other annuity contract types because it is the only annuity contract in which your money is subject to losses as a result of market declines. Your contract value has a greater opportunity to grow, but it also stands to lose. Additionally, your contract's value will be subject to the underlying investment's fees and limitations—including capital gains taxes, management fees, etc. Once it is time for you to receive income from the contract, the insurance company will pay you a certain income, locked in at whatever your contract's value was.

Variable annuities are, in my opinion, generally not the best vehicle available for use by consumers who are near or in retirement and need reliable income, and this is why we do not offer them. Variable annuities often come with higher fees than other products, usually in the range of 2-4 percent, and their built-in product features (such as a lifetime income) can usually be found in other annuity products without the added investment fees. Discussed in the following, fixed and fixed index annuities are, in our opinion, often better choices for preserving principal and lifetime income possibilities.

Fixed

A traditional fixed annuity is pretty straightforward. You purchase a contract with a guaranteed interest rate and, when you are ready, the insurance company will make regular income payments to you at whatever payout rate your contract guarantees. Those payments will continue for the rest of your life and, if you choose, for the remainder of your spouse's life.

Fixed annuities don't have much in the way of significant upside potential, but many people like them for their guarantees (after all, if your Aunt May lives to be ninety-five, knowing she has a check later in life can be her mental and financial safety net), as well as for their predictability. Unlike variable annuities, which are subject to market risk and might be up one year and down the next, you can pretty well calculate the value of your fixed annuity over your lifetime.

Fixed Index

To recap, variable annuities take on more risk to offer more possibilities to grow. Fixed annuities have less potential growth, but they protect your principal. In the last couple of decades, many insurance companies have retooled their product line to offer fixed index annuities, which are sort of midway between variable and fixed annuities on the risk/reward spectrum. Fixed index annuities offer greater growth potential than traditional fixed annuities but less than variable annuities. Like traditional fixed annuities, however, fixed index annuities are protected from downside market losses.

Fixed index annuities tie your potential growth to external market indexes, meaning that instead of your contract value growing at a set interest rate like a traditional fixed annuity, it has the potential to grow within a range. Your contract value is credited interest based on the performance of an external market index like the S&P 500 without ever being invested in the market. You don't invest in the S&P 500 directly, but the insurance company will credit your annuity contract based on the S&P 500's gains, up to a cap.

For instance, if your contract caps your interest at 5 percent, then, in a year the S&P 500 gains 3 percent as of your contract anniversary, your annuity value increases 3 percent. If the S&P 500 gains 35 percent, your annuity value gets a 5 percent bump. But, since your money isn't actually invested in the market with a fixed index annuity, if the market nosedives (2000, 2008, and 2020 anyone?), you won't see any increase in your contract value. Conversely, there will also be no decrease in your contract value (other than optional rider costs, if any)—no matter how badly the market performed, you won't lose any of the interest you were credited in previous years.

So, what if the S&P 500 shows a market loss of 30 percent? Your contract value isn't going anywhere. For those who are more interested in protection than growth potential, fixed index annuities can be an attractive option because, when the stock market has a long period of positive performance, a fixed index annuity might just enjoy a conservative gain in its value that usually has more upside potential than just offsetting the effects of inflation. And during stretches where the stock market is erratic and stock values across the board take significant losses? Fixed index annuities won't lose anything from the stock market volatility.

People like fixed index annuities because they offer principal protection from market loss coupled with the chance to earn a reasonable return. If you want, you can tack on riders, death benefits, and other options to meet your individual needs.

Other Things to Know About Annuities

We just talked about the four different kinds of annuity contracts available, but all of them have some commonalities as annuities.

For all annuities, the contractual guarantees are only as strong as the insurance company that sells the product, which makes it important to thoroughly check the credit ratings of any company whose products you are considering.

Annuities are tax-deferred, meaning you don't have to pay taxes upfront or on interest earnings as the contract value grows. Instead, you will pay ordinary income taxes on your withdrawals. These are meant to be long-term products, so, similar to other tax-deferred or tax-advantaged products, if you begin taking withdrawals from your contract before age fifty-nine-and-one-half, you may have to pay a 10 percent federal tax penalty. Also, while annuities are generally considered illiquid, most contracts allow you to withdraw up to 10 percent of your contract value every year. Withdraw any more, however, and you could incur additional surrender penalties.

Keep in mind, your withdrawals will deplete the accumulated cash value, death benefit, and possibly the rider values of your contract.

Taking a bucket approach to your portfolio, annuities are typically used to address the question, "Will I run out of money?" Few options out there provide guaranteed lifetime income, but annuities are one of them. Annuities can help ease retirees' worries. As long as they might live, retirees can have money coming their way if they have an annuity.

One guy I work with, I'll call him Bob, has been a super-aggressive investor throughout his working years. He's done exceptionally well in the stock market. But he didn't want to worry about market performance when it came to his regular lifestyle income.

For someone in a position like Bob's, taking a bucket approach that allows them to have income locked down for different periods of their life can also give them the freedom to have money set aside to invest aggressively if they prefer. It's a have-your-cake-and-eat-it approach that can let people invest freely without concern for lifestyle income.

Annuities aren't for everyone, but it's important to understand them before saying "yea" or "nay" on whether they fit into your plan; otherwise, you're not operating with complete information, wouldn't you agree? Regardless, you should talk to a financial professional who can help you understand annuities, help you dissect your particular financial needs, and help show you whether or not an annuity is appropriate for your retirement income plan.

CHAPTER 8

Estate & Legacy

In my practice, I devote a significant portion of my time to matters of estates. That doesn't mean drawing up wills or trusts or putting together powers of attorney or anything like that. After all, I'm not an estate planning attorney. But I am a financial professional, and what part of the "estate" isn't affected by money matters?

I've included this chapter because I have seen many people do estate planning wrong. Clients, or clients' families, have come in after experiencing a death in the family and have found themselves in the middle of probate, high taxes, or a discovery of something unforeseen (often long-term care) draining the estate.

Alternately, I have seen people do it right: clients or families who visit my office to talk about legacies and how to make them last and adult children who have room to grieve without an added burden of unintended costs, without stress from a family ruptured because of inadequate planning.

I'll share some of these stories here. However, I'm not going to give you specific advice, since everyone's situation is unique. I only want to give you some things to think about and to underscore the importance of planning ahead.

My office has strategic parnerships with a couple different law offices. One is a full-service firm with a slew of attorneys. They'll hold your hand through the process, and they host many seminars and informational presentations. The other firm is more nuts and bolts in nature. The head attorney of this firm will do what you need for a very reasonable price. Between our two partners, we have options to help satisfy your unique needs. Both are at the top of their field; they just go about working with clients in different ways with their differences appealing to different personalities.

You Can't Take It With You

When it comes to legacy and estate planning, the most important thing is to *do it*. I have heard people from clients to celebrities (rap artist Snoop Dog comes to mind) say they aren't interested in what happens to their assets when they die because they'll be dead. That's certainly one way to look at it. But I think that's a very selfish way to go about things—we all have people and causes we care about, not to mention those who care about us. Even if the people we love don't *need* what we leave behind, they can still be fined or legally tied up in the probate process or burial costs if we don't plan for those. And that's not even considering what happens if you become incapacitated at some point while you are still alive. Having a plan in place can greatly reduce the stress of those responsibilities on your loved ones; it's just a loving thing to do.

Documents

There are a few documents that lay the groundwork of legacy planning. You've probably heard of all or most of them, but I'd like to review what they are and how people commonly use them. These are all things you should talk about with an estate planning attorney to establish your legacy.

Powers of Attorney

A power of attorney, or POA, is a document giving someone the authority to act on your behalf and in your best interests. These come in handy in situations where you cannot be present (think a vacation where you get stuck in Canada) or, for durable powers of attorney, even when you are incapacitated (think in a coma or coping with dementia).

It is important to have powers of attorney in place and to appoint someone you trust to act on your behalf in these matters. Have you ever heard of someone who was incapacitated after a car accident, whether from head trauma or being in a coma for weeks—sometimes months? Do you think their bills stopped coming due during that time? I like my phone company and my bank, but neither one is about to put a moratorium on sending me bills, particularly not for an extended and interminable period. A power of attorney would have the authority to make sure your mortgage gets paid or your cable gets canceled while you are unable.

You can have multiple POAs and require them to act jointly.

What this looks like: Do you think two heads are better than one? One man, Chris, significantly relied on his two sons' opinions for both his business and personal matters. He appointed both sons as joint POA, requiring both their signoffs for his medical and financial matters.

You can have multiple POAs who can act independently.

What this looks like: Irene had three children with whom she routinely stayed. They lived in different areas of the country, which she thought was an advantage; one month she might be hiking out West, the next she could enjoy the newest off-Broadway production, and the next she could soak up some Southern sun. She named her three children as independently authorized POAs so, if something happened, no matter where she was, the child closest could step in to act on her behalf.

You can have POAs who have different responsibilities.

What this looks like: Although Luke's friend, Claire, a nurse, was his go-to and POA for health-related issues, financial matters usually made her nervous, so he appointed his good neighbor, Matt, as his POA in all of his financial and legal matters.

In addition to POAs, it may be helpful to have an advanced medical directive. This is a document where you have pre-decided what choices you would make about different health scenarios. An advanced medical directive can help ease the burden for your medical POA and loved ones, particularly when it comes to end-of-life care.

Right now, I have a client whose family sold their almond and pecan orchard. Her parents, who founded the farm, had seven children, all of whom are entitled to some of the inheritance. Unfortunately, one child is an addict. As you can imagine, while the parents want to provide their son the help he needs, they do not want to hand him a lump sum of money he may not be fit to handle. The only way for them to ensure their wishes are upheld is with a trust and POA.

Many families want their children to work hard and use their inheritance frugally. It's frustrating when I see clients pass away without having set up trusts or a POA, and, two months later, their children show up having bought luxury cars and fancy speed boats. I've seen inheritors burn through a lifetime of savings in a matter of weeks. What's most upsetting is all of that could have been avoided.

Wills

Perhaps the most basic document of legacy planning, a will is a legal document wherein you outline your wishes for your estate. When it comes to your estate after your death, having a will is the foundation of your legacy. Without one, your loved ones are left behind, guessing what you would have wanted, and the court will likely split your assets according to whatever the state's defaults are. Maybe that's exactly what you wanted, as far as anyone knows, right? Because even if you told your nephew he could have your car he's been driving, if it's not in writing, it still might go to the brother, sister, son, or daughter to whom you aren't talking.

However, it may not be enough just to have a will. Even with a will, your assets will be subject to probate. Probate is what we call the state's process for determining a will's validity. A judge will go through your will to question if it conflicts with state law, if it is the most up-to-date document, and if you were mentally competent at the time it was in order, etc. For some, this is a quick, easily-resolved process. For others, particularly if someone steps forward to contest the will, it may take years to settle, all the while subjecting the assets to court costs and attorney's fees.

One other undesirable piece of the probate process is it is a public process. That means anyone can go to the courthouse, ask for copies of the case, and discover your assets, as well as who is slated to receive what and who is disputing.

Some clients come to me with horror stories relating to this. When their parents died, creditors came out of the woodwork to claim owed money. Such people can force the probate process to drag on for years. There's even a whole industry of people who watch obituaries looking for individuals who might owe money somewhere.

It's also important to remember beneficiary lines trump wills. So, that large life insurance policy? What if, when you bought it fifteen years ago, you wrote your ex-husband's name on the beneficiary line? Even if you stipulate otherwise in your will, the company holding your policy will pay out to your ex-spouse. Or, how about the thousands of dollars in your IRA you dedicated to "children" thirty years ago, but one of your children was killed in a car accident, leaving his wife and two toddlers behind? That IRA is going to transfer to your remaining children, with nothing for your daughter-in-law and grandchildren.

That may paint a grim portrait, but I can't underscore enough the importance of working with a skilled estate planning attorney to keep your will and beneficiary lines up to date, for the sake of your loved ones, as your life changes.

Trusts

Another piece of legacy planning to consider is the trust. A trust is set up through an attorney and allows a third party, or trustee, to hold your assets and determine how they will pass to your beneficiaries. Many people are skeptical of trusts because they assume trusts are only appropriate for the fabulously wealthy.

However, a simple trust may only cost $1,000 to $2,500 in attorney's fees and can avoid both the expense and publicity of probate, provide a more immediate transfer of wealth, avoid some taxes, and provide you greater control over your legacy. [42]

For instance, if you want to set aside some funds for a grandchild's college education, you can make it a requirement he or she enrolls in classes before your trust will dispense any funds. Like a will, beneficiary lines will override your trust conditions, so you must still keep insurance policies and other assets up to date.

––––––––––––––––––––––––––

[42] Regan Rondinelli-Haberek. LegalZoom. "What is the Average Cost to Prepare a Living Trust?" https://info.legalzoom.com/average-cost-prepare-living-trust-26932.html

Like any financial or legal consideration, there are many options these days beyond the "yes or no" of having a trust. For one thing, you will need to consider if you want your trust to be revocable (you can change the terms while you are alive) or irrevocable (can't be changed; you are no longer the "owner" of the contents). A brief note here about irrevocable trusts: While they have significantly greater tax benefits, they are still subject to a Medicaid look-back period. This means, if you transfer your assets into an irrevocable trust in an attempt to shelter them from a Medicaid spend-down, you will be ineligible for Medicaid coverage of long-term care for five years. Yet, an irrevocable trust can avoid both probate and estate taxes, and it can even protect assets from legal judgments against you.

Another thing to remember when it comes to trusts, in general, is, even if you have set up a trust, you must remember to fund it. In my eight years' work, I've had numerous clients come to me, assuming they had protected their assets with a trust. When we talk about taxes and other pieces of their legacy, it turns out they never retitled any assets or changed any paperwork on the assets they wanted in the trust. So, please remember, a trust is just fancy legal papers if you haven't followed through on retitling your assets.

One of my clients has a daughter and son who were the beneficiaries of their aunt's estate (my client's sister). The aunt had set up a trust and named the trust as the beneficiary . . . but *only for one account.* It took a good year of work, phone calls, and letters to straighten out the legal process when she passed away. Eventually, the money made its way to the right place, but, unfortunately, it was a much smaller sum than it could have been, since a portion of the inheritance was spent in taxes. That could have been avoided. Her mistake was thinking action taken in respect to one account would cover all her other accounts because they were all managed under one custodian. But that's not how things work. In fact, each account must be handled individually.

Taxes

Although charitable contributions, trusts, and other tax-efficient strategies can reduce your tax bill, it's unlikely your estate will be passed on entirely tax-free. Yet, when it comes to building a legacy that can last for generations, taxes can be one of the heaviest drains on the impact of your hard work.

For 2017, the federal estate exemption was $5.49 million per individual and $10.98 million for a married couple, with estates facing up to a 40 percent tax rate after that. In 2020, those limits have increased to $11.58 million for individuals and $23.16 million for married couples, with the 40 percent top level gift and estate tax remaining the same. Currently, the new estate limits are set to increase with inflation until Jan. 1, 2026, when they will "sunset" back to the inflation-adjusted 2017 limits.[43, 44] And that's not taking into account the various state regulations and taxes regarding estate and inheritance transfers.

One frequent tax concern: retirement accounts.

Your IRA or 401(k) can be a source of tax issues when you pass away. For one thing, taking funds from a sizeable account can trigger a large tax bill. However, if you leave the assets in the account, there are still required minimum distributions (RMDs), which will take effect even after you die. If you pass the account to your spouse, he or she can keep taking your RMDs as is, or your spouse can retitle the account in his or her name and receive RMDs based on his or her life expectancy. Remember, if you don't take your RMDs, the IRS will take up

---

[43] Ashlea Ebeling. Forbes. December 21, 2018. "Final Tax Bill Includes Huge Estate Tax Win for the Rich: The $22.4 Million Exemption."
https://www.forbes.com/sites/ashleaebeling/2017/12/21/final-tax-bill-includes-huge-estate-tax-win-for-the-rich-the-22-4-million-exemption/
[44] Ashlea Ebeling. Forbes. November 6, 2019. "IRS Announces Higher Estate And Gift Tax Limits For 2020."
https://www.forbes.com/sites/ashleaebeling/2019/11/06/irs-announces-higher-estate-and-gift-tax-limits-for-2020/#18b9e5652efb

to 50 percent of whatever your required distribution was, plus you will still have to pay income taxes whenever you withdraw that money. Thanks to rules enacted in 2020, anyone who inherits your IRA, with few exceptions (your spouse, a beneficiary less than ten years younger, or a disabled adult child, to name a few), will need to empty the account within ten years of your death.

Also—and this is a pretty big also—check with an attorney if you are considering putting your IRA or 401(k) in a trust. An improperly titled beneficiary form for the IRA could mean the difference of thousands of dollars in taxes. This is just one more reason to work with a financial professional, one who can strategically partner with an estate planning attorney to diligently check your decisions.

Some families feel legacy planning condemns them to be seen as unloving, making them look like they believe their beneficiaries would not be able to sort things out on their own after they pass. Everyone would like to think they can work things out fairly after a family member passes away, but, take it from me, planning in advance does not mean your family doesn't love each other. For example, I have three siblings. When we're together, we can't even decide on a place for dinner. Can you imagine how hard it would be to make decisions that really count under the stressful circumstances of a death in the family?

One couple I worked with passed away three or four years ago. They'd been proactive about planning for their kids. Every few years we would have brief meetings with the whole family when the kids were in town for holidays. When the dad passed away, it had been decided in advance some money would go to the kids.

Money can bring out the worst in people. The more comprehensive the legacy plan, the better you can preserve familial ties and ensure that, after the losing a loved one, you don't have the added burden of navigating finances.

Finding a Financial Professional

My mom had two jobs when I was a kid—a newspaper route when we were little and part-time work helping some finance guys. That was my first exposure to the industry. My mom would show me papers with examples of how saving little bits of money over time with a reasonable return could achieve impressive growth. I always loved math and finance, so things like that astounded me. As I grew older, I would help my mom's employers around the office, and occasionally they'd let me sit in on client meetings. I started to realize they weren't really planners; they just pushed life insurance policies. Still, in concept, I liked what they were doing, or at least what they purported to do. But, I felt too young at the time to manage people's assets. So, I took several years to learn the industry from the inside out. I worked for various companies in every corner of the financial world, and, finally, in 2012, I felt confident I was ready to open my own practice.

Over the years, I've acquired much of the licensing and qualifications you may recognize if you've already looked into finding a financial advisor. I have passed the Series 65 securities exam, meaning I hold a securities license, as well as an insurance license in many states. However, I really pride myself on my communications degree. Growing up around finance workers, I was told time and again the most valuable quality in an advisor is the ability to succinctly, clearly, and simply explain to clients what they ought to do. There are many advisors involved in making a plan but few who can communicate it well.

In many respects, a good financial advisor is like a good doctor. He or she must be good at their job, and they must convey to you what you need to do in a way that allays your potential fears and concerns. A financial advisor and a doctor have something else in common, too—they each perform a function people should not undertake by themselves. No one would try to perform self-surgery just to save a few bucks—that should be obvious. In the same way, I believe that people should not make weighty financial decisions without professional help.

Some people think retirement planning is just about pricing mutual funds. If that was the case, I would say "do it yourself, it's not that hard." But, a retirement plan should be so much more. Financial planning involves true diversification of assets and the skill to coordinate all the moving parts of your portfolio. It also outsources the challenge and stress of ensuring lifetime income. Many clients say I'm also like a therapist because part of my job is to help clients prepare to enjoy retirement without concern over their financial state.

Remember, too, retirement today is nothing like it was for our parents. So much has changed. Pensions are largely nonexistent. We live in an extremely low interest rate environment (you used to be able to "safely" house much of your savings in CDs or bonds, but that doesn't work well these days). Longevity has behooved the modern retiree to create many extra years of income. Market researchers say the stock market is more volatile now than it has ever been. Health care is not as straightforward as it was in years past, and our tax situation is poised to change dramatically in the future. All these factors, and more, make retirement planning a more challenging undertaking than it has ever been. So, how can you select an advisor who can help guide you to a confident retirement?

First of all, explore several options. Interview potential advisors. Make sure they're independent—that means they can be objective. Look for those who operate under the fiduciary standard of care. That means they are legally required to act in your best interest when providing investment advice. Make sure they can perform comprehensive planning, not just insurance and annuity sales. I would also recommend you find an advisor with a team. Some do it on their own, but it's hard to run a business all alone while also maintaining the highest quality of work on the client's behalf.

There are many great advisors out there. People often interview advisors looking to see who has the best investments, but no advisor has the right investment for everyone's situation, every time. What you really want is an advisor who views money the same way you do, who shares your ideals and perspective. After all, your advisor will be a partner for the rest of your life. Make sure you find someone who complements your personality and shares similar goals.

After checking off the list of "must haves," be careful, also, to look for red flags. One big red flag is a combative personality. I've seen some advisors get fired up if you don't do things their way. Those probably aren't the kind of people you'll want to deal with for the next thirty years. Another potential problem to watch for is if an advisor is solely interested in the return on your money. That may sound good at first, but it's a narrow perspective that often gets people in trouble—remember, as we've discussed throughout the book, lower returns with less risk much of the time are often a better option than high returns that come with high degrees of risk. Also, an advisor who says there's only one way to do things might just be revealing he or she just doesn't know another way to do it. A good advisor can work with your opinion; it's your money after all. Beware of the dogmatic advisor.

Last, but not least, you must consider how an advisor is paid. Some advisors are fee-based, and they should disclose if they also get additional commission on some products. Ideally, you want someone with different payment options to match your circumstances. At my office, we have some clients who do most of their own advising and just want to come in for a meeting or two a year and pay a reasonable fee for consultation. Others are totally hands-off, so their payment structure is different. Regardless of how an advisor gets paid, make sure the services you receive are of commensurate value. Investment services are important, but they are not the whole bag, and they don't usually take very much time. Larger-scale planning services, on the other hand, can be time consuming and often more valuable.

Fees should be reasonable but not cheap. If you want the cheapest price, you'll likely get the cheapest services. That's a basic truth that applies in all areas of life. At the same time, the most expensive option is not necessarily the best. At some point there isn't much extra an advisor can do to justify exorbitant fees.

As I write this book in 2020, the stock market and economic climate is in chaos. But that has only convinced me I took the right career path. It wouldn't be rewarding to me if I only helped people make more money. But, to help people pursue their goals and to live happy lives? That's fulfilling. Each successive story from my clients affirms my love of this job.

If you live in the area and you need help planning for retirement, please, give my office a call. I would love to chat with you. I feel like I'm good at taking your dream or your vision and plotting a realistic course to help you reach it. As people near retirement, they often express that they're tired and unable to work for something that may not be possible. I can often help clients make it possible, and my team can do the footwork to save you energy and put you on the path to help reach your goal.

I can sum up my goal for people at or near retirement in two points. One: I want to help them retire sooner than they thought was possible or, at least, show them it is possible, whether they want to retire or not. Two: For those who are retired, I want to help them live their best life while they have the health and energy to do it.

Money should never be the reason you don't live out your dreams. Health and energy aren't as easy to control, but I don't want you to consider money as a limiting factor to pursuing your goals. Most people work their entire lives with retirement as the prize at the end of the road. Make it count. Plan for retirement *the right way* and enjoy the life you've always wanted.

Acknowledgments

To anyone and everyone that has supported me through this journey. To my mother, Judy, who taught me the value of hard work by getting me up in the morning to throw newspapers. To my father, Ace, who taught me how to support a family. To Sherri for helping me build this business. To my children for always loving me. To Jeff and Derek for providing me an opportunity. To Advisors Excel for showing me the right way to do things. To all my clients for your trust and confidence. To Garrett for taking a leap of faith. And to everyone else that has shown me there is *more* to life than just paying bills and losing weight!

About the Author

Chad Ensign is a financial advisor focused on helping clients work toward their retirement dreams through a well-thought-out strategy for retirement income. He founded his independent company to better serve clients by providing a wide range of insurance and investment products.

As a child, Chad enjoyed working with numbers and was gifted in math. He was introduced to the world of financial services at a young age through friends and family. He grew to love teaching others the importance of managing their money. However, the financial world Chad was introduced to was a captive insurance firm, meaning Chad could only offer his clients the limited products and services that the parent company offered. Chad wanted to give his clients a broader range of products to choose from to help them decide which options best fit with their individual situations.

Now the head of his own independent firm, Chad enjoys sharing his knowledge with clients to help them understand how to make their money work for them. His philosophy is to enjoy your money while you have the health and energy to do so.

Chad has passed the Series 65 exam and is an Investment Adviser Representative. He also holds the Retirement Income Certified Professional (RICP) designation. He holds life and health insurance licenses in several states, but his primary focus is in Arizona, Utah, and California (operating with California Insurance Licence No. 0K68065). Chad earned his bachelor's degree in communications from California State University at Sacramento. He is also a contributing author to *Kiplinger* online.

Away from the office, Chad enjoys spending time with his four children. He coaches his kids' sports and enjoys boating and being outdoors. His family lives in Mesa, Arizona.

www.ingramcontent.com/pod-product-compliance
Lightning Source LLC
Chambersburg PA
CBHW071532150726
48000CB00002B/771